The Brownsville Affair

KENNIKAT PRESS

NATIONAL UNIVERSITY PUBLICATIONS

SERIES IN AMERICAN STUDIES

General Editor

JAMES P. SHENTON

Professor of History, Columbia University

ANN J. LANE

The Brownsville Affair

National Crisis and Black Reaction

NATIONAL UNIVERSITY PUBLICATIONS
KENNIKAT PRESS
PORT WASHINGTON, N.Y. · LONDON · 1971

Library of Congress Catalog Card No.: 73-139357
ISBN 0-8046-9008-1

Published by
Kennikat Press, Inc.
Port Washington, N.Y./London

*for my father
and
the memory of my mother*

ACKNOWLEDGMENTS

Many friends and colleagues gave generously of their time and thought, and it is a pleasure to be able to thank them now.

John Hope Franklin first interested me in the subject many years ago when I was his research assistant and he was chairman of the history department at Brooklyn College; as friend and teacher he has given unfailing guidance, encouragement and warm support from those first stages of my research to the present. Richard Hofstadter directed the study as a dissertation and provided, as all knew him will affirm, a congenial atmosphere of respectful independence which I very much appreciated. Eugene D. Genovese read the full manuscript more than once and offered, as always, incisive and important criticisms. Phyllis Dain and Norman Dain also read the manuscript entirely, and I profited enormously from their extended comments. My brother Lawrence Lane and his wife, Patricia Lane, both mathematicians and grammarians, brought their precise skills to my assistance. To Warren I. Susman my debt is unending.

Susan Kaplan and Peter Kuznick, former students of mine at Rutgers University, helped me in the final stages of research, and Anita Beckerman assisted me with the index. The accuracy of portions of the book was much improved by the close reading given by Seth Scheiner and Gerald Grob.

My husband, William H. Nuchow, whose talents and interests take him into the world where, he once said, history is made and not written, did not type the manuscript, tend the children or wash the dishes, but he was there when I needed him during those dark and terrible times.

CONTENTS

Part I – The Incident

Part II – The Black Community

Part III – The National Political Scene

The
Brownsville
Affair

PART I

THE INCIDENT

INTRODUCTION

A few minutes before midnight on August 13, 1906, a group of men, probably from ten to twenty, ran through the streets of Brownsville, Texas, and fired into buildings, seemingly at random. A bartender in the Ruby Saloon, named Frank Natus, was killed, and the lieutenant of police, M.Y. Dominguez, was wounded and had his horse shot from under him. Another citizen by the name of Paulino S. Preciado, the editor of a newspaper published in Spanish, *El Porvenir*, claimed to have been slightly injured by a bullet grazing the back of his hand.

Companies B,C, and D of the First Battalion of the United States Infantry, colored, under the command of Major Charles W. Penrose, were at the time stationed at Fort Brown, just outside of Brownsville. The black battalion had arrived on Saturday, July 28, and had been there just two weeks and two days when the shooting occurred. Even in that short time, however, relations between the local whites and the black soldiers had deteriorated. Two fairly serious and one trivial incident had occurred in which soldiers were accused of behaving disrespectfully to the townspeople and for which they were physically assaulted. The day of the raid there was a complaint issued, but never investigated because of the raid, that a soldier had attempted to rape a white woman in Brownsville.[1]

"Other circumstantial evidence linked the soldiers with the raid. The area attacked was adjacent to the enlisted men's barracks in Fort Brown and was separated only by a low wall. Empty shells along the route of attack were immediately assumed to have been fired from the new Springfield rifles. Most

5

damning were the allegations made to a local citizens' committee by several
Brownsville townspeople that they recognized, either by sight or by voice, the
raiders to be Negro soldiers."[2]

The shooting was the subject of many investigations, and it soon assumed national importance well beyond the merit of the incident itself. What
might have remained a small episode was projected into the political arena by
Senator Joseph Benson Foraker of Ohio, who mobilized the widespread and
profound outrage of the black community into a lengthy but ultimately
unsuccessful campaign against President Theodore Roosevelt. In the process,
Foraker attempted to forge a movement to assist him in wrenching the presidential nomination from Taft, Roosevelt's choice, in 1908. Not only did
Foraker fail in his presidential ambitions, but largely as a result of his opposition to the President on the Brownsville issue, Roosevelt drove him from
political life. The more Foraker was able to expose Roosevelt's mishandling
of the Brownsville issue, the more determined was Roosevelt to exact permanent payment for the humiliation.

The black community underwent serious dislocation as a result of the
Brownsville issue. The split, which had in 1905 resulted in the establishment of the anti-Booker T. Washington Niagara Movement, forerunner to the
National Association for the Advancement of Colored People, sharpened
appreciably. Washington's unwillingness to criticize Roosevelt publicly, although he privately opposed the President's actions, induced many previous
Washington supporters to flee to the radical camp. On the Brownsville issue
the division soon became one not between radicals and moderates but between those committed to the Republican party and everyone else. In the
short run Washington emerged the victor, for as the political implications of a
split with the President became apparent and as Washington brought increasing pressure on the recalcitrant, the threat of political disaffection at the polls
collapsed. But the loss to the Washington camp of many outstanding and
outspoken black leaders was permanent.

The Brownsville raid occurred during a period, said Mr. Dooley, "when
the negroes had been fully deprived of the homely privileges of dependence in
exchange for the dubious gift of civil rights — unshackled in Virginia so's he
[sic] could be lynched in Ohio."

There is grim irony in the disagreement among historians as to what date
marks the lowest point in the history of Afro-Americans. Rayford Logan's
description of the nadir as the period 1877-1901 has provoked discussion as
to whether a later date would be more appropriate. Most agree that the point
falls somewhere in the first decade and a half of this century just preceding
the great migration to the cities.[3]

Racial segregation, established by law, had appeared during Reconstruc-
tion but disappeared shortly after. As C. Vann Woodward has demonstrated,

soon after the first Jim Crow law was passed by Tennessee in 1875 the rest of the South followed. By the end of the century the black American was barred from white hotels and theaters and restaurants, as well as from churches and schools.

"The South's adoption of extreme racism was due not so much to a conversion as it was to a relaxation of the opposition. . . .The restraining forces included not only Northern liberal opinion in the press, the courts and the government, but also internal checks imposed by the prestige and influence of the Southern conservatives, as well as by the idealism and zeal of the Southern radicals. What happened toward the end of the century was an almost simultaneous—and sometimes not unrelated—decline in the effectiveness of restraint that had been exercised by all three forces: Northern liberalism, Southern conservatism and Southern radicalism."[4] As the United States undertook its imperialist adventures and accepted the White Man's Burden, Woodward has suggested, she took up at the same time many Southern attitudes on the subject of race.

As the new century wore on blacks learned that they not only kept the old difficulties but added some new ones. Increasingly, both blacks and whites moved into urban areas, in the North and South, with the black job seekers securing only the least attractive employment. At least part of the difficulty came from the discriminatory American Federation of Labor and a hostile white organized labor movement in general.

Soon everyone was to realize that for the black the new century not only meant considerable more bloodshed, but bloodshed of a qualitatively different kind as well. If the number of lynchings declined from more than 150 in each of the peak years of 1892 and 1893 to the 60's and 70's after 1908[5], two significant changes had occurred. The proportion of lynchings occurring in the South increased at the same time that the proportion of lynched victims who were white decreased. "In other words, lynching was becoming an increasingly Southern and racial phenomenon."[6]

In addition, race riots began to replace lynchings as methods of repression and expressions of hatred. Such riots increased rapidly in number and barbarity from the Wilmington, North Carolina riot in 1898 and the New York riot in 1900 to the Atlanta holocaust in 1906.

John Milholland, a white reformer, claimed that the Negro's condition was worsening each year.

> He is standing on the very threshold of a physical slavery almost as bad and hopeless as that from which he was emancipated. . . .Practically a political serf in a dozen states, without right to vote or liberty to speak; trial by jury of his peers denied him, and in such imminent danger of lynching that he lives under a reign of terror as awful as that inspired by Ku Klux depredations or the old Spanish inquisition.[7]

In a country with a tradition of lawlessness and violence, the nationwide attitude toward the blacks was solidifying into a hostility of such intensity as had not been previously known. Even Senator Ben Tillman of South Carolina could state to the United States Senate that "race hatred grows day by day ... the South is occupying an attitude of constant friction, race riot, butchery, murder of whites by blacks and blacks by whites, the inevitable, irrepressible conflict."

Although the white residents of Brownsville undoubtedly shared the notions about blacks with those of their section, and indeed their nation, there were only a handful of black residents in the town at the time of the raid. Brownsville had some 6,000 residents, probably two-thirds Mexican. As a result there was a decidedly Spanish, as well as Southern, quality to the town.

Brownsville is at the bottom of the Rio Grande Valley, the southern-most point in the United States. Located on the Rio Grande River at the border, it is immediately opposite Matamoros, Mexico. Although Browns-ville is today a very poor community,[8] it was not always so. Its story goes back to the Mexican War when General Zachary Taylor established a base at the site from which he fought the battles of Palo Alto (May 8, 1846) and Resaca de la Palma (May 9, 1846). "The general changed the name of the post from Fort Taylor to Fort Brown in honor of Mayor Jacob Brown, who died defending it during the second battle." Fort Brown gave its name to the tiny civilian settlement.[9] Brownsville became the county seat of newly created Cameron County in December 1848, and in January 1850 the town was incorporated.

In 1848 at the close of the war, Charles Stillman, an enterprising pro-moter, planned a town adjoining the government fort, "bought up the little steamboats used by Taylor's transport corps and established a regular passen-ger and freight service to the head of navigation, which was sometimes Rio Grande City and sometimes Roma." Just at the time the steamboat went into operation, gold was discovered in California. The gold rush gave Brownsville a boom that lasted for a decade. "The would-be miners came off the ships at Point Isabel (since called Port Isabel) and flooded Brownsville by the thou-sands to buy supplies at the local trading posts and to await transportation on Stillman's paddle boats." Some apparently tired of waiting for the boats. Others probably were attracted by the sight of so much cash business and stayed behind. Many remained to work with Charles Stillman and his son, James, "to build a fortune that was to be the basis of a large banking house."[10]

The Brownsville boom continued for some years after the California rush had slowed because many of the valley dwellers, including a few of Stillman's pilots, went into the cattle business. In seven years ranching had become big business, with all of the inherent difficulties. There were the typical problems of cattle production, such as access to markets, ownership of ranges, and thievery. "As the industry grew larger, so did the influence of the cattle owners." And there seems to have been a "rather casual attitude" toward the property rights of Mexicans who had deeds to considerable tracts north of the river.

The Civil War almost made Brownsville a metropolis. Because of its isolated position as the southernmost point in the United States, it immediately became one of the most important seaports of the Confederacy. "Out onto the Gulf the little paddle boats of the King and Kenedy Line hauled cotton, wool and hides to European ships anchored three miles offshore." Back they came with medical supplies and arms and ammunition. The traffic was year round. Prices were high and money easy. Many in the area became prosperous, and the men who risked the running of steamboats out onto the Gulf were accumulating large fortunes.[11]

With the growth of the railroad network, Brownsville ran into difficulties. Railroads reached San Antonio in the 1870's and pushed on to Laredo by 1881. El Paso was reached by 1883. At Laredo, the rails made contact with Mexico, and both El Paso and Laredo, then tiny towns, began to grow rapidly. Brownsville, which had been the "queen city of the Rio Grande, was now bypassed." Struck also by a yellow fever epidemic, Brownsville stagnated. Its northern capitalists drifted elsewhere. The lower river valley "retreated into a stunted cattle culture."[12]

In the early years of the century, businessmen in the Brownsville area made a renewed effort to revitalize their community. In the Southwest in general there was a new development of massive agriculture and the processing of agricultural products. In Texas, the combination of a widened railroad network, organized land companies and "extensive and expensive irrigation projects invaded the old cattle enclaves along the Rio Grande." Truck farming developed enormously. Tons of vegetables, fresh and canned, were shipped North by rail. Towns and cities grew — all based on Mexican labor. "None of it would or could have taken place without a great mass of low-paid workers from south of the Border"[13]

Brownsville made a desperate effort to participate in this new agricultural activity. By the time of the raid, the St. Louis, Brownsville and Mexico Railroad was established, but it came too late to remake Brownsville. One of Brownsville's most influential residents, Judge James B. Wells, Jr., leader in the local Democratic party, worked hard at rebuilding Brownsville's importance. A wealthy corporation lawyer and the son of a prominent cattle rancher, Wells was largely responsible for the railroad that was built through Brownsville. He served as its attorney-general for many years. He was prominent in promoting the international bridge across the Rio Grande at

Brownsville.[14] George Brulay, a Brownsville businessman, amassed a fortune in the cane-growth business, and through experimentation demonstrated the great capacity of the Brownsville area for the growth of sugar cane.[15]

The greatest effort at boosting Brownsville came from *The Brownsville Daily Herald*, the only newspaper published in Cameron County. Articles appeared regularly describing the unlimited business opportunities in Brownsville, the rich alluvial soil, and the prosperity of truck farming in the surrounding territory. "Settlers are pouring in from the North," said the editor, Jesse O. Wheeler, three weeks before the raid. The editor focused criticism on three groups of Brownsville residents who, he claimed, hindered the town from prospering. Those who held the waterworks and electric light franchise and had done nothing about it were a disgrace. "There is not another town in the United States," Wheeler asserted, "that is not provided with these utilities and be it said to our everlasting shame that this can be said of our city."[16] Also to be criticized was he who persistently "knocks the town where he resides." The editorial offered a new version of the Ninth Commandment: Thou shalt not bear false witness against the town wherein thou dwellest, but speak well of it to all men.[17] The third element was the large landowner. Proprietors come here, the editor informed his readers, and they come at the rate of a half dozen or more a day, but they find very little land for sale. All along the line lands are being placed on sale, "and here we sit doing nothing. . . . How long will our land owners . . . retard the progress of the Brownsville section?"[18]

In the midst of this anguished and desperate effort to recreate the old prominence- and prestige of Brownsville came the raid of August 1906 that brought instead notoriety and nationwide criticism.

NOTES

1. U.S. Senate, 59th Cong., 2d sess., Doc. 155, pt 1, Vol. XI, ser. no. 5078 *Report on Brownsville Affray*. Hereafter cited as *Report on Brownsville Affray*.
2. James A. Tinsley, "Roosevelt, Foraker and the Brownsville Affray," *The Journal of Negro History*, XLI (January, 1956), p. 44.
3. See the preface to Rayford W. Logan, *The Betrayal of the Negro: From Rutherford B. Hayes to Woodrow Wilson*, originally published as *The Negro in American Life and Thought: The Nadir, 1877-1901* (New York: Collier Books, c. 1954, 1965).
4. C. Vann Woodward, *The Strange Career of Jim Crow* (New York: Oxford University Press, 1955), p. 51-52. For further discussion see chap. 11.
5. *Crisis*, IX (January, 1915), 3, as quoted in August Meier, "Negro Racial Thought in the Age of Booker T. Washington, circa 1880-1915" (unpublished Ph.D. dissertation, Columbia University, 1957, 2 vols.), p. 497.
6. C. Vann Woodward, *Origins of the New South, 1877-1913*, Vol. IX of *A History of the South* (Baton Rouge: Louisiana State University Press, 1951), p. 352.

7. Address to *National Negro Conference* (New York: 1909), pp. 128-29.
8. In 1968 Brownsville was one of the two lowest per capita income urban areas in the United States. T.R. Fehrenbach, *Lone Star: A History of Texas and the Texans* (New York: The Macmillan Company, 1968), p. 666.
9. Robert J. Casey, *The Texas Border* (New York: The Bobbs-Merrill Co., Inc., 1950), p. 385.
10. *Ibid.*
11. *Ibid.*, p. 386.
12. Fehrenbach, p. 605.
13. *Ibid.*, p. 688.
14. The Texas State Historical Association, *The Handbook of Texas*, Walter Prescott Webb, Editor-in-Chief (Chicago: The Lakeside Press, 1952), II, 878.
15. L. E. Daniell, *Texas: The Country and Its Men* (1917), p. 501.
16. *The Brownsville Daily Herald*, July 19, 1806, editorial, p. 2.
17. *Ibid.*, July 23, 1806, editorial, p. 2.
18. *Ibid.*, July 25, 1806, editorial, p. 2.

I

THE RAID

The First Battalion of the United States Twenty-fifth Infantry, together with other companies of the regiment, had been previously stationed at Fort Niobrara, Nebraska, for more than two years, and had earlier served in the Philippines, in Cuba, and on the frontier. When the troops went to Brownsville they relieved a battalion of the Twenty-sixth United States Infantry — white soldiers who had been there for almost two years.

Originally the black troops were scheduled to go first to Austin, Texas, in time to participate in maneuvers to be held at Camp Mabry, in Austin, on July 20. "But the officers of the Twenty-fifth, all white, protested strongly in letters sent to the Adjutant of the battalion."[1] Captain J. C. Leitch said that while he was stationed at Fort Sam Houston from November, 1899 to July, 1900:

> the men of this company, and of other companies of the regiment stationed with them, were subjected to continual persecution by the citizens of San Antonio on account of their color. Soldiers quietly walking along the streets were ordered by policemen to get off the sidewalks..., these orders being accompanied invariably with vile and abusive language. Soldiers were arrested and confined in city jail on charges so trivial that the courts would not convict them of any offense....Company D, Twenty-fifth Infantry, stationed at Fort McIntosh, had similar experiences, the trouble finally culminating in an

12

attack upon the troops. . . .

In my opinion the sentiment in Texas is so hostile against colored troops that there is always danger of serious trouble between the citizens and soldiers whenever thay are brought in contact. The hostility of a regiment of Texas National Guard toward the Twenty-fifth Infantry at the maneuver camp at Fort Riley in 1903 was so marked that it was considered necessary to take measures to defend the camp of the regiment against an attack which was threatened by said Texas regiment.[2]

Several other officers wrote similar letters discussing the tensions earlier between the Texas militia and the Twenty-fifth. Typical of many other statements, Captain Michael J. Lenihan wrote that, in his opinion, the War Department should rescind the order directing the Twenty-fifth Infantry to proceed to Austin for maneuvers. He thought it important to

avoid a repetition of the condition of affairs that existed during the maneuvers at Fort Riley, Kans., in 1903, when a regiment of Texas Militia occupied the camp contiguous to that of our regiment. . . .

Due to race prejudice, and without provocation, the individuals composing the Texas regiment, officers and men, frequently insulted our soldiers, and were it not for the excellent discipline that existed in our regiment and the soldierly fortitude with which our men bore the gibes and insults of the Texas Militia, the consequences might have been serious. . . .

Our officers and men at that time retained their self-control under trying circumstances. Can the War Department, if it puts them again, knowingly, in a similar disagreeable position and throws them, advisedly, in contact with this unfriendly militia, hope that trouble will be avoided? Judging from our past experience, is the outcome of this encampment liable to reflect any credit on either the United States or Texas?[3]

Second Lieutenant Donald D. Hay reported that Texas troops "hissed and jeered" at the Negro soldiers when they passed.

The commander at Fort Niobrara, Nebraska, in a statement sent to the Military Secretary at San Antonio, went beyond the question of maneuvers when he wired:

Request that Twenty-fifth Infantry not be sent to Maneuvre Camp, Austin, Texas, and that if possible the regiment be stationed in some section of the country where race prejudice is less violent than in the South.[4]

Upon receipt of these and other similar requests, the War Department rescinded the order sending the troops first to Austin.

In Brownsville, news of the transfer of a black battalion to that city was received May 27, 1906. "Complaints soon began to reach Washington from

Brownsville citizens requesting that the orders be changed."[5] Senator Charles A. Culberson of Texas forwarded to the War Department a letter he had received from a U. S. Commissioner stationed in Brownsville. The Commissioner, S. P. Wreford, advised that the War Department order replacing the white troops with black ones was "a very unfortunate move at this time for B'ville while we have so many prospectors coming who are looking for locations." Wreford concluded that "the Border is a poor place to station negro soldiers."

Secretary Taft's response was illuminating:

> The fact is that a certain amount of race prejudice between white and black seems to have become almost universal throughout the country, and no matter where colored troops are sent there are always some who make objection to their coming. It is a fact, however, as shown by our records, that colored troops are quite as well disciplined and behaved as the average of other troops. . . .The records of the Army also tend to show that white soldiers average a greater degree of intemperance than colored ones. It has sometimes happened that communities which objected to the coming of colored soldiers have, on account of their good conduct, entirely changed their view and commended their good behavior to the War Department.[6]

There is considerable evidence to indicate that there was a good deal of threatening and angry talk generally throughout the community of Brownsville as soon as it was discovered that the black trooops were to be sent to Fort Brown to replace the white troops.

Captain Benjamin J. Edger, Jr., of the Medical Department, testified that "the expressed sentiment of the people was that they did not like colored troops and would not have them." When pressed for the names of individuals he quoted Captain Kelley as having said, " 'The people of this town don't like colored troops; they don't want them here.' " Captain Edger went on to quote Dr. Combe, the Mayor, who had said that although he found black troops satisfactory, " 'These people will not stand for colored troops.' "[7]

First Sergeant Nelson Huron, a white soldier in the Twenty-sixth Infantry, stationed at Brownsville, stated that in general "the people of Brownsville were prejudiced against the United States uniform," and that specifically he heard many comments in Brownsville unfriendly to the coming of the black soldiers. He referred to statements made by Mr. Weller, a Brownsville saloonkeeper, that " 'he did not want these colored soldiers to come there, and that no one in Brownsville wanted them to come there, and that he did not think they would stay there very long when they did come.' " Mr. Weller, according to the white soldier, later said that the people "would get rid of them some way before long. . . .He did not say anything about how they would get rid of them. . . .Possibly that day he heard Mr. Weller tell some one

THE RAID   15

else that 'the citizens were going to get up an appeal'. . .to be sent to their
Congressmen and to Senators Bailey and Culberson."

Sergeant Huron also spoke of a conversation he had had with a Mr.
McDonald who, he said, asserted that " 'The people in Brownsville don't want
them damned niggers here, and they won't have them here.' "[8]

Second Lieutenant Edwin P. Thompson, another white officer of the
Twenty-sixth Infantry, testified the following:

> many derogatory remarks were made. . .by some citizens in reference to
> the colored soldiers in words as follows: ". . .We don't want them damn
> niggers here; Niggers will always cause trouble."[9]

A San Antonio resident, L.H. Printz, stated that while standing on the
railroad platform at Hildalgo, Texas, he overheard some Brownsville citizens
threaten to "shoot over the barracks to keep the negro soldiers" out.[10] A
former dining room orderly of Company M of the Twenty-sixth Infantry,
William J. Rappe, swore that after it was known that the black soldiers were
coming to Brownsville he heard Policeman Fernandez, in the presence of
many witnesses, say that "If the colored soldiers came there all they had to
do was to kill a couple of them and you would get rid of them again."[11]

Mayor Combe, on the other hand, who had previously served with black
troops and knew Captain Macklin, one of the company commanders of the
Twenty-fifth, "found colored troops well disciplined and anticipated no
trouble." He ordered the Brownsville police to show the black soldiers the
same consideration as white troops.[12] In general, Mayor Combe insisted, he
heard no expressions of hostility to the impending arrival of the black soldiers
among the townspeople in Brownsville.[13]

Despite the ominous atmosphere in which the troops arrived, relations
between local residents and the soldiers proved to be better in some respects
than anticipated. Artificer George Newton, of Company D, related that he
was told by a local drug store attendant that the soldiers were "the nicest set
of boys" he had ever met.[14] Friendly relations between Mayor Combe and
the officers of the battalion tended to encourage an atmosphere of harmony.

Two of the four saloons owned by white residents established separate
bars in the rear for the black soldiers. The other two saloons barred the
troops. The four other saloons owned by Mexicans welcomed the soldiers. A
recently discharged soldier of the Twenty-fifth, William Allison, and Private
John Holloman, who financed the business, set up a bar to accommodate the
soldiers. This saloon began operation on August 9, four days before the riot
occurred.

But in the sixteen days before the raid there were three altercations, two
of them serious, that caused public concern.

The two incidents, referred to frequently during the months of investigations, were the Tate-Newton case and the Baker-Reed case. The Tate-Newton case involved a party of ladies standing on a street sidewalk. They claimed that two black soldiers rudely jostled them. Fred Tate, inspector of customs, husband of one of the ladies, knocked down one of the soldiers with his revolver. According to a later government report, the ladies were obstructing the sidewalk, although anybody could easily have walked by them. The soldier was rude and probably insulting in his manner, the report claimed, but Tate's remedy, somewhat drastic, was "in the manner of the South."[15] Tate insisted that he would have responded identically to any such rudeness, whether from a black man or white. The collector of customs invited the commander of the post, Major Penrose, to assist in an investigation of the case, but there was no time after August 13.

The soldiers claimed that the assault upon James W. Newton was un-provoked. According to Newton, the incident took place on Sunday evening between 8:00 and 9:00 p.m., while he was taking a walk with Private Frank J. Lipscomb. "As we passed beyond the post office," he said, "there was a party of ladies that we had to walk by in file in order to pass them, and as I passed them I said something to Frank — I have forgotten what it was — and when I looked around this way again, why, someone had drawn back, and as I turned that way he struck me with a revolver and knocked me down." His friend, Lipscomb, confirmed his story.[16]

Captain Macklin, of C Company, described Newton's reaction to the incident. He was not incensed or angry but he felt hurt. "Newton was a splendid soldier. . .and I do not believe, knowing the man, that he would deliberately pass any people on the sidewalk, white or colored, and brush against them or knock them off." He had been Macklin's company clerk for some time and "was extremely polite and obedient."[17]

Later Tate had been heard bragging about the attack, Captain Macklin said, and he, Macklin, then undertook an investigation that seemed to satisfy Newton completely. In any case, said Macklin, Newton never even learned the name of the man who struck him.[18]

The second altercation involved two soldiers, one named Oscar W. Reed, who were at the ferry landing, having just returned from Matamoros. The inspector of customs, A. Y. Baker, claimed they were drunk and disorderly, which the government report said was confirmed by unprejudiced witnesses, that Baker told them to move on, and finally pushed one, who fell off the plank into the mud and water about knee-deep, more because of his condi-tion than the strength of the push, although Baker probably used "more force than he acknowledged," the report asserted. The government investigator concluded that the "facts in these two cases were exaggerated on both sides and increased the bitter feeling between soldiers and citizens."[19] Reed did admit that he had been drinking and was noisy and he was glad to let the matter drop. He was, in general, said Captain Macklin, a "happy, good-natured sort of man."[20]

Another small incident that reflected the attitude of some of the townspeople toward the soldiers concerned Private Clifford Adair who came from Matamoros with a little silver pen. A customs official stopped him at the border with the words: "Here. I will not allow any nigger to bring anything over here. You are smuggling." There was no duty on the item.

It was also claimed that on the night of the shooting a soldier assaulted a Mrs. Evans and that the people of Brownsville grew greatly incensed, but there seems to have been no credible evidence supporting such an accusation. Apparently the rumors did arouse a great deal of excitement among the citizens of Brownsville, because Mayor Combe called upon Major Penrose later that day, at 5:00 p.m., told him about the alleged assault and advised him to keep his men in quarters that night on the grounds that they might be harshly dealt with by the citizens, should they be seen in town. Mayor Combe's exact language was: ". . . Then I made use of one or the other of these expressions: 'Major, if you allow these men to go into town to-night I will not be responsible for their lives,' or 'Major, do not allow your men to go out of the post, because there is a great deal of danger in town.' "[21]

The details of the raid apparently can be reconstructed as follows. The raiders, in number up to twenty, met at the entrance to Cowen Alley, a narrow passageway between Elizabeth and Washington Streets. Across the street was a low fence that separated Fort Brown from Brownsville. A volley of shots was fired presumably near the garrison wall. The raiders then ran up Cowen Alley, firing indiscriminately at buildings. Louis Cowen's house, in which Mrs. Cowen and her five children were asleep, was hit first, the bullets striking low enough to have seriously endangered the family. As the men proceeded up the Alley they encountered the police lieutenant, shot at him and killed his horse. After several more rounds of shots, the raiders divided into two groups. The first group continued through the Alley, and when they neared the Ruby Saloon, fired into it, killing the barkeeper and perhaps wounding Paulino Preciado. The second group turned left on Washington Street, where they shot into the home of Fred E. Starck. The raid was over. Although there was conflicting testimony concerning the duration, it probably lasted about ten minutes.[22]

The loud reports of the rifle fire quickly awakened many of the town's residents. Mayor Combe ran from his home toward the scene of the firing. As he approached Twelfth Street, he was warned by one of the city policemen to go no farther, that ". . .the Negroes are shooting up the town. . . ."[23] The Mayor walked into a nearby saloon and was again told by a group of men that the black soldiers were creating the disturbance. By that time the firing had ceased. As the rumor swept the town that the soldiers were responsible, resentment and anger grew. Groups of men began to accumulate. Most of the men were armed. There was talk about charging the fort, but Mayor Combe urged the men to disperse, pointing out to them the foolishness of a small group of ill-equipped men attempting to storm a fort held by three companies of armed and trained soldiers.

Inside the fort, Major Penrose and his men thought the post had been attacked and he immediately posted a command in a defensive position along the garrison wall. Not until a detachment of soldiers, sent to town to investigate the shooting, had returned to the fort with Mayor Combe, was Penrose aware that the townspeople thought the soldiers were guilty. Penrose was amazed and skeptical, but since Mayor Combe was not only the acting post surgeon but also a man of great integrity and sympathy, he checked the men and the weapons. He found no incriminating evidence.

Shortly after daybreak Mayor Combe returned with fifty or sixty empty Army rifle shells found along the line of attack. It was only then that Major Penrose and his officers, Second Lieutenant George Lawrason (B Company Commander), Captain E. A. Macklin (C Company Commander), Captain Samuel P. Lyon (D Company Commander), and Lieutenant Harry S. Grier (Quartermaster and Commissary of the post), were convinced that the men were indeed guilty, although further questioning did not reveal which of them had been involved.

In town, meanwhile, the Mayor appointed a committee of four who were to appoint, in turn, a committee of fifteen to conduct an investigation of the raid and to carry on negotiations with Major Penrose. Of the four men chosen by the Mayor, two were ex-Federal officers of the Civil War. Captain Kelley, later chosen head of the Citizens' Committee, was an ex-officer and one of the town's leading citizens. E. H. Goodrich, the superintendent of public schools, was a Republican and also a retired Federal officer. William Ratcliff, a director of the First National Bank and president of the Brownsville Land and Irrigation Company, and James A. Brown, a large landowner in southwest Texas, were the other two selected to appoint a committee.[24]

The Citizens' Committee (also called the Committee on Safety) was formed and Captain Kelley elected chairman.

It began its investigation the day after the raid and heard the testimony of many Brownsville citizens. The statements were not made under oath, but they were reported stenographically. At that time the occurrences of the previous night were presumably fresh in the minds of the witnesses.

The Committee operated on the assumption, as did all of the witnesses, that the shooting had been done by black soldiers. The inquiry was directed toward determining which of the soldiers were guilty.

For example, Herbert Elkins was called to the stand:

Q. You know the object of this meeting. We know that this outrage was committed by negro soldiers. We want any information that will lead to a discovery of who did it.[25]

Another witness was told:

Q. We are inquiring into the matter of last night with a view to ascertaining who the guilty parties are. We know they were negro soldiers. If there is anything that would throw any light on the subject we would like to have it.[26]

Twenty-two witnesses, all Brownsville citizens, appeared before the Committee, but only eight identified the rioters as black soldiers. Five of these eight witnesses asserted that they saw the raiders and recognized them as Negro soldiers. The three remaining witnesses testified that they heard the raiders as they ran through the alley and recognized them by their voices as blacks.[27]

It seemed to the citizens of Brownsville so natural that the soldiers were guilty that the statements of the witnesses were not challenged.

On August 15, after a two-day investigation, the Citizens' Committee telegraphed President Roosevelt:

Our condition, Mr. President, is this: Our women and children are terrorized and our men are practically under constant alarm and watchfulness. No community can stand this strain for more than a few days. We look to you for relief; we ask you to have the troops at once removed from Fort Brown and replaced by white soldiers.[28]

President Roosevelt responded immediately. Secretary of War Taft was vacationing and therefore was not officially informed of the riot by his office until August 22. Meanwhile President Roosevelt on August 16 ordered an immediate investigation and specified that the troops remain in Brownsville until the investigation was completed. Major August P. Blocksom, Assistant Inspector-General of the Southwestern Division, arrived in Brownsville to assume charge of the investigation.

The citizens of Brownsville remained unsatisfied at the continued presence of the troops and wired President Roosevelt again requesting their removal. Major Blocksom also recommended the removal of the troops, which was done, and their replacement by white troops, which was not. But by August 25 the battalion was en route to Fort Reno, Oklahoma Territory, where Blocksom completed his investigation.

In the meantime the civil authorities in Texas were taking action. On August 23 Judge Welch of the Twentieth Judicial District issued warrants for the arrest of twelve members of the black battalion on charges of murder and conspiracy to murder. The twelve had been selected by Captain William McDonald of the Texas Rangers, who had been permitted to question the troops at Brownsville. The group, which included three sergeants, three corporals and six privates, was made up of the most likely suspects. It included: William Allison, who had been discharged from Company B and had opened a saloon for the men of the battalion; Sgt. Brawner, in charge of Company C quarters; Cpl. Powell, in charge of Company D quarters; Sgt. Reid, sergeant-of-the-guard on duty at the time; Cpl. Miller, from Company C, on a pass at the time of the shooting; Cpl. Madison, corporal-of-the-guard; Pvt. Howard, the sentinel on post between the barracks and the reservation; Pvt. Newton, the soldier assaulted by Tate; Pvt. Reed, the soldier pushed off the plank into the water by Baker; Pvt. Askew, who was thought to be the owner of a soldier's cap found in the streets the morning after the shooting; and Pvt. Holloman, from Company C, who owned a part of the Allison saloon.

Concerning the reasons for the selection of these particular men, General McCaskey noted that "the manner by which their names were procured is a mystery. As far as is known there is no evidence that the majority of them were in any way directly connected with the affair. It seems to have been a dragnet proceeding."[29]

It was believed by the civil authorities investigating that there were circumstances pointing to these men. It was assumed, and perhaps rightly, that it would have been impossible for a conspiracy to have been organized, the guns to have been secured from the gun racks, and the shooting party to have gone into town and to have returned without the noncommissioned officers in charge of the quarters having some knowledge of the affair, without the sergeant- and corporals-of-the-guard having some knowledge and without the sentinel on duty having some knowledge. It was thought in the absence of any other motive that the shooting must have had relation to the offenses committed against Pvt. Newton and Pvt. Reed and that consequently they would have had some knowledge of it. It was assumed that the saloon established for the troops was the center of the conspiracy and therefore the two owners must have had some knowledge of the raid.

The men were confined to the Fort Brown guardhouse. When the other troops left for Fort Reno, the twelve suspects were removed to Fort Sam Houston in San Antonio.

The case was presented to the Grand Jury for Cameron County, Texas, of which Brownsville is the county seat, at its September session. After three weeks of investigation it was found there was no evidence on which to base an indictment of anybody. As far as civil authorities were concerned the twelve were entitled to release. They were retained until after the Fort Reno investigation and then given the same punishment as their comrades.

On August 29 Major Blocksom filed his report. "That the raiders were soldiers of the Twenty-fifth Infantry can not be doubted," he said.[30] At the same time he asserted that the commanding officers and some of the senior noncommissioned officers could not be held responsible for not discovering "the preconcerted raid." As the officers firmly believed, until the next morning, that the garrison had been attacked, the raiders were not suspected by their officers and had no difficulty in returning to their positions.

Although the officers are sincerely attempting to locate the criminals, it is unfortunate, he went on, that they have as yet discovered so few clues. The battalion "had an excellent reputation up to the 13th of August, but the stain now upon it is the worst I have ever seen in the Army." Many of the old soldiers must have some knowledge of the guilty parties, Blocksom contended, and if they do not disclose their knowledge "they should be made to suffer with others more guilty, as far as the law will permit."[31]

He recommended that if satisfactory evidence concerning the identity of the criminal was not forthcoming by a certain date, that "all enlisted men of the three companies present on the night of August 13 be discharged from the service and debarred from reenlistment in the Army, Navy and Marine Corps."[32]

He concluded his report: "It must be confessed the colored soldier is much more aggressive in his attitude on the social equality question than he used to be."[33]

Roosevelt accepted Blocksom's recommendation. Major Penrose, who had been holding his own investigation from the beginning, continued to have no success in identifying the culprits. In view of the failure, Major Penrose proposed two alternative plans to help discover the guilty men. First, he suggested that all restrictions be removed and the men be allowed full liberties, but that three detectives be assigned, one to each company, to discover the guilty parties. An alternative suggestion was that the Secretary of War be granted the authority to discharge 80 per cent of the enlisted personnel of the three companies. The men were to be told that unless the guilty members were identified by a certain date, 20 per cent of each company was to be discharged each month until either the guilty men were produced or until the battalion reached a strength of only 20 per cent of its original number.

Neither plan was adopted. On October 4, Roosevelt ordered General E. A. Garlington, the inspector general, to Fort Reno and to Fort Sam Houston, where the twelve suspects were being held. The President directed him "to secure information that will lead to the apprehension and punishment of the men of the Twenty-fifth Infantry believed to have participated in the riotous disturbance which occurred in Brownsville, Texas."[34] Garlington was authorized to make known to the soldiers that unless those who had knowledge of the raid and its participants came forward, every man in the three Companies of the Twenty-fifth Infantry would be discharged without honor.

On October 22, 1906, eighteen days after receiving the assignment, General Garlington made his report. After first consulting with Major Blocksom, who had made "an exhaustive investigation,"[35] he went to Fort Sam Houston to examine the men in the guardhouse, for whom warrants had been issued immediately after the raid. He examined each of the prisoners carefully, engaging them in general conversation about family and background, but as soon as the matter of Brownsville was raised "the countenance of the individual being interviewed assumed a wooden, stolid look, and each man positively denied any knowledge in the affair."[36] Further, no individual admitted that the discrimination and abuse the soldiers suffered caused any feeling of animosity toward the citizens of Brownsville. When General Garlington became convinced that no information would be obtained, he again called the men before him and told them of the President's order. He gave them until 5 o'clock that afternoon. He received no information.

He then went on to Fort Reno, Oklahoma, where he discovered that the officers had not been able to find out anything from their men. He repeated his earlier method, called before him the soldiers individually, but received the same denial and the same "mental attitude." The unanimous denial "indicated a possible general understanding among the enlisted men of this battalion as to the position they would take. . .but I could find no such evidence of such understanding. The secretive nature of the race, where crimes charged to members of their color are made, is well known."

He concluded:

It has been established, by careful investigation, beyond reasonable doubt, that the firing into the houses of the citizens of Brownsville. . .was done by enlisted men of the Twenty-fifth Infantry. . . .

General Garlington recommended that as soon as practicable, every man in Companies B, C, and D be discharged without honor and forever debarred from reenlisting in the armed service or from employment in any civil service position. In making the recommendation, Garlington admitted many men who had "no direct knowledge" of the riot would suffer. But as they "appear to stand together in a determination to resist the detection of the guilty, therefore they should stand together when the penalty falls. A forceful lesson should be given to the Army at large, and especially to the noncommissioned officers," he said.[37]

In the early weeks of the investigation only one official report, that of Lieutenant Colonel L.A. Lovering, submitted on October 4, included sworn statements from the soldiers themselves. He examined, he said, all the witnesses available at Fort Reno, and particularly carefully those who had had difficulties with the townspeople. He put to each of the witnesses several questions, which they answered. The questions almost all concerned where the individual was the night of the raid, which soldiers were recognized while the firing was going on, what problems existed between any given soldier and the people of Brownsville, what complaints, if any, were heard expressed by the soldiers in the days the troops had been stationed at Fort Brown. Almost all of the soldiers denied any knowledge of difficulty between soldiers and civilians. Most of the soldiers asserted that they had been asleep when the firing began and that their assumption was, when awakened by the shooting, that the garrison was being attacked. The affidavits were attached to Lovering's report. Several of the soldiers testified to having heard derogatory expressions such as "Black sons of bitches" while the firing was going on.[38] Several of the soldiers claimed to have seen and heard men firing at the fort.

Major Blocksom, after examining the affidavits, added his comments. He said that although a number of men were positive that shots were fired toward the post, their statements being based on flashes from rifles and sounds of bullets, he could "find no evidence of bullets striking anywhere on the post, and none has yet been given."[39] He also heard nothing of the epithets the soldiers said were hurled at the fort. He further noted that the affidavits containing those assertations were made at least a month after the raid. Finally, nobody in B Company heard any such expressions, although those quarters were much nearer the firing than C Company's.

By November 5, Roosevelt had read Garlington's report, agreed with the findings, and instructed his Secretary of War, William Howard Taft, to carry out the recommendation. Execution of the order began November 16, and ten days later the last member of the battalion was discharged from the United States Army.

NOTES

1. Tinsley, "The Brownsville Affray," p. 9. For greater details of the raid see especially Chs. I and II.
2. *Report on Brownsville Affray*, pp. 1665-1666.
3. *Ibid.*, p. 1667.
4. U.S. War Dept., Off. Adj. Gen. Mil. Sec. Off., *Brownsville File*, July 7, 1906.
5. Tinsley, " The Brownsville Affray," p. 12.
6. *Report on Brownsville Affray*, p. 1610.
7. *Ibid.*, p. 2116.
8. *Ibid.*, p. 2117-18.
9. *Ibid.*, p. 2119.
10. *Ibid.*, p. 2120-21.
11. *Ibid.*, p. 2121.
12. *Ibid.*, p. 2029.
13. *Ibid.*, p. 2412.
14. *Ibid.*, p. 143.

24   THE BROWNSVILLE AFFAIR

15. U.S. Senate, 60th Cong., 1st sess., Report No. 355, pt. 1, Vol. II,
    Report of the Senate Committee on Military Affairs, p. 61.
16. *Ibid.*, p. 2959.
17. *Proceedings of a General Court-Martial. . .in the Case of Major Charles W. Penrose*,
    p. 543.
18. *Report of the Senate Committee on Military Affairs*, p. 1784.
19. *Ibid.*, p. 62.
20. *Ibid.*, p. 3125.
21. *Ibid.*, p. 2382.
22. *Court of Inquiry Proceedings*, p. 2159.
23. *Report of the Senate Committee on Military Affairs*, p. 1784.
24. *Ibid.*, pp. 2393-94.
25. *Ibid.*, p. 85.
26. *Report on Brownsville Affray*, p. 446.
27. *Ibid.*, p. 445.
28. *Ibid.*, p. 21.
29. *Ibid.*, p. 66.
30. *Ibid.*, p. 427. Full report contained on pp. 425-430.
31. *Ibid.*, p. 428.
32. *Ibid.*, p. 429.
33. *Ibid.*, p. 430.
34. *Ibid.*, p. 109.
35. *Ibid.*, p. 3. Full report contained on pp. 3-8.
36. *Ibid.*, p. 4.
37. *Ibid.*, p. 7.
38. *Ibid.*, p. 111. Full report contained on pp. 110-177.
39. *Ibid.*, p. 177.

II

THE CONSTITUTION LEAGUE

Again the seal is broken and a name
   is added to the list, by Justice kept.
Of Heroes in the cause of righteous fame
   Where Ethiopia's bleeding heart has wept.

. . . The cause of right can never be defiled,
   But lives untainted 'mid the blackest spurn,
For truth and facts are weapons ever styled
   To bless the wielding hand in which they turn.[1]

In the weeks following Roosevelt's order, no one publicly challenged the assumption of the guilt of at least some of the soldiers of the Twenty-fifth Infantry. What was examined, and then either defended or criticized, was the harshness of the order affecting 167 men. But on December 10, 1906, the Constitution League, a civil rights organization, submitted a report to the United States Congress stating that the evidence indicated that the Brownsville soldiers were innocent; and thereby began the entire investigation.

The Constitution League was an interracial organization formed shortly before the Brownsville affray to attack disfranchisement and other forms of discriminatory practice by means of court action, legislation, and propaganda. Its leading spirit was John E. Milholland, a prosperous manufacturer of pneumatic tube equipment and a Progressive Republican politician with interests

25

in reform, peace, and women's suffrage.

In an interview in London, Milholland, with characteristic zealousness, described the Constitution League as:

> a belated expression of the American conscience, an effort at last to organize in comprehensive, effective manner the country's latent moral and patriotic sentiment... the League represents the banding together throughout the Union of citizens . . .who are determined that the Constitution of the United States shall not become permanently, as it is at present, a mere sectional document – dead, so far as regards suffrage conditions in the South.

Milholland went on to discuss the "disgraceful truth" that so demoralized was public sentiment in the white South and so indecisive had northern opinion become, that in most southern states the Constitution was "trodden under foot," and the Supreme Court had practically avoided the question by insisting that the matter was one for Congress, not the Courts.

In view of the fact, Milholland continued, that there had been three lynchings a week for the past ten years in the South and that the entire black electorate – all native-born citizens – of the South was disfranchised by force or fraud, it was clear that the Constitution had not been zealously safeguarded by the Courts.

The Constitution League proposed that immediate action should come from Congress and that wherever a state had denied to its citizens the right to vote, it was the duty of Congress to reduce the base of representation to the basis "which the number of such male citizens shall bear to the whole number of male citizens of 21 years of age in such State."

Milholland optimistically foresaw success for such a bill within a short time, for the Republican party, he believed, was committed to its passage. He felt that politically the northern Negroes were too crucial to ignore. Theodore Roosevelt owed his political life to the black vote, Milholland insisted, for without the 30,000 black votes in the state of New York he would never have been elected to the Governorship, and therefore probably never would have been chosen for Vice President. If the black vote had been suppressed throughout the country in previous presidential elections, as it was then in the South, Grant would have been defeated in 1868, Hayes in 1876, Garfield in 1880, Harrison in 1888, and McKinley in 1896. By defeating Bryan in 1896 the Negro vote "prevented a result which would have ruinously affected Europe and America, and saved the country from the crime of free silver, for which the whole South stood solidly."

The existence of the League, Milholland concluded, and the hopes which it aroused among the Afro-American community was the one great insurance that the nation possessed against the outbreak of a war of races. The black

people keep hoping that constitutional rights might be constitutionally vindi-
cated. "If they were once to feel themselves deserted . . . I guess that despair
would unlock the gates of Hell."[2]

The Constitution League report, for all of the haste and passion it revealed, had the effect of provoking more detailed study of the President's
action. Senator Foraker later stated that the report of the Constitution
League induced him to call for a full Senate investigation.[3]

After Foraker discovered the Constitution League, he worked closely
with it throughout the months of the Senate hearings. At the beginning of the
Senate investigation, for example, Foraker informed Milholland that the
Senate Committee had rejected the League's offer to provide an attorney for
the soldiers. Without the presence of a legal representative from the League,
Foraker wrote, he would depend upon N.B. Marshall and Gilchrist Stewart,
two black Constitution League attorneys, to give such additional information
"as I may need to enable me to act intelligently in the selection of witnesses."
It might even be necessary, Foraker added, "to call upon you."[4]

Foraker was involved closely, too, with the financing of the League's
activities. Milholland was the heaviest contributor, complaining in his diary
that he had underwritten the cost of most of the initial investigation carried
on by Stewart in preparation for the League's report.[5] But Foraker also
helped the Brownsville investigation carried out by the League after its initial
report. At one point Milholland apologized to Foraker for the long-standing
debt of $500 that the League owed him and suggested that they establish a
subscription list with twenty-five men each pledged to contribute $1,000.
"You have spent a great deal of money yourself," he commented to Foraker,
and while "I know you do not begrudge it, what is comparatively a trifling
affair to twenty-five becomes a burden to one or two."[6] The cost of running
the headquarters Milholland estimated to be between $400 and $500 a
month. "The colored contributions do not yet amount to $1,000; not one-
sixth of my personal donations," Milholland complained.[7] Foraker answered
by return mail, assuring Milholland that the indebtedness of the League to
him need give him no concern; in fact, he had already written to Stewart
committing himself to further expenditures. The suggestion of a subscription
is a good one, he said, but if "I could talk with you I could explain better
than I can by letter why I fear it is impossible to accomplish results that
way."[8]

Milholland was not drawn to the case originally out of a belief in the
innocence of the soldiers. An entry in his diary of November 18 indicates that
at that time he assumed some of the soldiers were guilty.

> The week has been spent trying to save the Negro soldiers in Texas
> whom President Roosevelt has ordered to be dishonorably discharged
> because they refused to "peach" upon their comrades who shot up

Brownsville to avenge the insults inflicted upon them by the local Bourbons.

Just eleven days later, on November 29, a four-page statement was submitted to Theodore Roosevelt by the League's attorney, Stewart, and with Milholland's approval, maintaining the likelihood of the soldiers' innocence and outlining a case which was a skeletal version of the final report issued a month later.[9]

On December 11 Foraker introduced a petition from the Constitution League which "respectfully memorializes the Congress to institute an inquiry relative to the discharge 'without honor' " of the three companies on the basis of the League's preliminary report which "seems to indicate that the riot of August 13 was neither created by nor participated in by members of the above companies."[10]

The League's report, which was based largely on published Government documents, pointed out emphatically the assumption of guilt made by all the investigating agencies: the Citizens' Committee, which was a "wholly irresponsible body without authority to administer an oath";[11] and the Government investigators. Blocksom, Garlington, and Lovering.

Blocksom's report showed, said the League, and the few men he examined corroborated it, that he was biased. Before he had even completed his investigation, the report went on, he had recommended disbandment of the three companies. Blocksom also claimed that the time from the call-to-arms to the roll call was at least ten minutes and probably longer, although Major Penrose and Captain Lyons officially stated that it was five minutes. The affidavits of men and noncommissioned officers showed it may have been eight minutes, but no more.

Blocksom also ventured the dubious statement, "sound of call-to-arms ordered by sergeant-of-the-guard probably too early during the fighting to be genuine." In fact, said the League, Musician Robinson sounded the call-to-arms by order of Major Penrose instantly, and the men fell in line at once and during the firing. Blocksom asserted that the soldiers jumped the walls, raided the town, fired into the homes of citizens, and, sustaining no injury to themselves, returned to the fort, escaping the observation of officers, and answered roll call. The roll calls of the three companies, verified by the officers, all of whom were white, showed that all the men were accounted for. To vindicate the Government verdict of guilt would require men equipped "with such miraculous speed and invisibility of persons as to get back over the stone walls to their companies. . .without being detected by the commissioned and noncommissioned officers."[12]

The League described Blocksom's assertion that the black soldier was "more aggressive" than he used to be as a reflection, not of the truth of the statement, but of the bias of the author.

Inspector-General Garlington, said the Constitution League, also began with the assumption that the soldiers were guilty. He restricted the few men he examined to answering questions related to identifying the culprits, the report said, but he refused to listen to any explanations by the soldiers concerning their innocence.

Both Blocksom and Garlington justified the discharge of the men in the guardhouse under lock and key and those sick in the infirmary. They justified the discharge of the men asleep in the officers' quarters while they exonerated the commissioned officers in the same houses. The privates were discharged, said the League; the officers were neither discharged, court-martialed, nor reprimanded.[13]

The Constitution League's report also pointed out that the instructions given to Garlington, dated October 4, assumed the guilt of some of the soldiers, despite the fact that Lovering's report, also dated October 4, which included the men's sworn testimony, could not have been examined either by Garlington or by the President, for the report had not yet reached Washington.

Major Penrose stated that it was the damaging evidence of the empty shells and used clips that convinced him that his men were implicated. The ease with which this evidence can be discredited, the League report claimed, made it amazing that Major Penrose should ever have been impressed by it. First, any common rifle could carry the Government cartridges if they were fired one at a time. Second, any number of cartridges and clips could have been picked up on the target practice grounds or secured by the dozen from the men or from the boxes in which they were stored. The Twenty-sixth Infantry had not long since finished target practice and had scattered, as was the practice, dozens of clips and cartridges as souvenirs and had allowed citizens free access to the boxes of discharged cartridges in the fort.[14]

Some of the officers who accepted without question the unsworn statements of Brownsville citizens should have realized, the League suggested, that it was probably too dark to see faces or uniforms. And the garments described by the eyewitnesses could well have been the khaki trousers or blue shirts almost universally worn in that vicinity, "particularly by the class of men likely to be present in any physical commotion."[15] In addition, the khaki uniform was worn officially by the police of Brownsville and frequently by the Texas Rangers, the League investigation uncovered.

One of the soldiers reported that at the time of their arrival at Fort Brown

> all the old uniforms — coats, pants and caps — were discarded and thrown upon the dune pile back of the quarters, and the Mexican and white boys from 7 on up, and the men as well, would come and gather up the old clothes that were thrown away, and you could see some of

them upon the streets of Brownsville, with uniforms on that they picked up, and to a person not knowing, you would think they were soldiers; and the stuff that was thrown away had the name of each soldier marked thereon.[16]

Two important eyewitnesses did not see any soldiers, the League report said, although they were in a position to if indeed the soldiers were responsible for the assault upon the town. William Voschelle, employed by the United States Government at Fort Brown, swore that he was sleeping in town on the night of August 13, was aroused by the firing, dressed hastily and headed for the post. He did not meet a single soldier on the way, but did meet four citizens dressed khaki uniform with arms, talking about the soldiers, and two policemen. Mathias Tamayo, the Mexican scavenger employed by the post, also swore that he saw no soldiers nor heard any shots fired from any of the company barracks, but that the shots came from outside the wall.

The League report returned frequently to the normal legal protections which were not respected: no cross-questioning of witnesses, no legal safeguards, no examination of the evidence as if in a courtroom, no presumption of innocence. The Constitution League challenged the right of Captain McDonald of the Texas Rangers to access to the fort. It was amazing, said the civil rights group, that the military authorities of the fort permitted a citizen, whatever his rank or reputation, to hold twelve soldiers for practically three months without any evidence against them. Even that Grand Jury, recruited from localities and communities from which judicial impartiality in a case against blacks was difficult to expect, could find no evidence upon which an indictment might be based.

How then did the Constitution League recreate the events of August 13? The report described in some detail the hostile feelings shared by many Brownsville citizens toward the soldiers. The evidence indicates that the citizens of Brownsville, or a certain element of them, were anxious to cause trouble for the soldiers. Sgt. Walter McCurdy[17] testified that Pvt. John Cook, who was stationed at outpost No. 2, acting as corporal, reported to him that he had seen civilians taking guns out of a frame building across the street from the barracks at 2:00 o'clock in the afternoon on August 14, the day McCurdy was sergeant-of-the-guard of the outpost duty. McCurdy told Cook to report the incident to the commanding officer. There was no mention of the incident in the Government report.

Musician Hoyt Robinson, on the night of August 13, after he was relieved as musician-of-the-guard, at about 2:00 o'clock in the morning, saw a number of citizens walking around the fort wall with guns.[18] There was no mention of this in the Government report.

John H. Hill testified that on August 14, between 1:00 and 2:00 o'clock in the morning, while on guard duty at post No. 6, he saw six or more citizens around the fort magazine, and that he sent Pvt. James Sinkler to report the occurrence to Sgt. Harris, commander-of-the-guard. Sinkler returned with Pvt. James Smith, and the three investigated. They found a magazine lock broken open, and in the door was an iron wedge, where an attempt had been made to pry it open. These facts were reported to the commanding officer of the day. There was no mention of this in the Government report.

All of these affidavits, as well as the trend of the evidence in general, the report claimed, indicated that an element existed in Brownsville intent upon creating serious trouble, perhaps attacking the soldiers.

All the Government case showed, the League contended, was that a party of men was engaged in a sudden "shooting up" of some part of the town — an occurrence common enough in frontier localities. The War Department case even provided a possible motive — the destruction of a new saloon operated by a recently discharged soldier. Fear that this enterprise might become profitable might have been the object of the assault. All of the indications that these varied motives existed, the report pointed out, came from an analysis of the depositions that had not yet arrived in Washington when the conclusion of guilt was embodied in the order of October 4.

The action taken by the Government, the Constitution League said, was based upon the biased opinions of the investigating officers and was not founded upon the testimony. There was, in fact, "fair reason" to believe that the commotion was created by civilians, partly to gratify a long harbored hatred against black soldiers and partly to punish their independence in boycotting the town's Jim Crow drinking saloons.

The report ended with a request for a congressional investigation by a committee empowered to summon and examine witnesses and report remedial legislation.

The Constitution League got its congressional investigation.

NOTES

1. Poem by Lucian B. Watkins, Joseph B. Foraker papers, Ohio State Historical Society, Cincinnati.
2. "Black Suffrage and White Sentiment," an interview with Milholland in the *Review of Reviews*, London, reprint in John E. Milholland papers, Fort Ticonderoga Historial Society.
3. Joseph B. Foraker, *Notes of a Busy Life* (Cincinnati: Stewart & Kidd Co. 1916), II, 234.
4. January 24, 1907, Foraker papers.
5. December 2, 1906, Milholland papers.
6. July 11, 1907, Foraker papers.
7. *Ibid.*

8. July 12, 1907, Foraker papers.
9. Communication to Roosevelt from Stewart, Milholland papers.
10. *Inquiry Relative to Certain Companies of the Twenty-fifth United States Infantry, issued by the Constitution League*, p. 1.
11. *Ibid.*, p. 3.
12. *Ibid.*, p. 9.
13. Although two of the officers were later court-martialed, the League's accusation in substance remains.
14. *Ibid.*, p. 15.
15. *Ibid.*, p. 3.
16. Affidavit L from Sgt. Jacob Frazer, *ibid.*, pp. 27–28. General Garlington did not question him.
17. Affidavit N, *ibid.*, p. 29.
18. Affidavit F, *ibid.*, p. 23.

III

THE SENATE HEARINGS

Of governor who's slow to act
  When minutes mean to die or live;
Of people's servants loath to move,
  And of a chief executive
Who asks for full particulars
  Of "that" and "this," the "how" and "why,"
Say, have we time for all of this
When hours may mean to live or die?

Say have we time! Your wife or mine,
  Your child or mine — your prattling child —
Crouched in the dread of awful things
  Our daughters murdered and defiled
Black fingers crooked about fair throat
  The leering field — the tortured breath —
Where's time for laggard red tape now,
When moments may mean life or death?

We of the South have known it long;
  The brooding horror we have known!
The black and mouthing, leering fear,
  When we our loved ones leave alone!

And shall the beast be armed and set
  Above us, left to break his will
On us, and our defenseless ones?
His only dream to rape and kill?

Justice! we ask, and speedily!
  Remove this incubus, and now!
Safeguard our homes, then hesitate,
  Then question "When?" and "Where?" and "How?"
If minded, till the crack of doom!
  Or tell us, "No!" that we may know
That to our strength we must look,
With our own arms give blow for blow!

And we will act! Aye, we will act!
  By all we love and we revere,
For wives with horror-haunted eyes!
For prattling babies more than dear!
For daughters more than sweet and fair!
  For them we'll fall, or for them stand!
Justice! we ask not any more —
By God we ask not! We DEMAND![1]

The Warren Majority Report

The Senate Committee on Military Affairs began taking testimony on the Brownsville case on February 4, 1907, and continued until June 14, 1907. Meetings were again resumed November 18, 1907, and concluded March 10 the following year. One hundred sixty witnesses were brought before the committee and testified under direct and cross examination. While there was considerable contradiction in the testimony, the majority of the members concluded that it pertained to irrelevant and immaterial points. The majority report concluded that:

1) The shooting in the affray at Brownsville was done by some of the soldiers belonging to the Twenty-fifth United States Infantry then stationed at Fort Brown, Texas.

2) The testimony did not identify the particular soldier or soldiers who participated in the shooting.

The following facts had, in the opinion of the committee, been "proven and established" and were issued in a brief report, under 10 pages, commonly referred to then as the Warren Majority Report (the report was named for Republican Senator F. E. Warren, a member of the investigating committee).

At approximately midnight on August 13, a number of soldiers armed with the new model (1903) Springfield rifle and Government ammunition, then in use in that battalion, jumped over the wall of the Government reservation separating the post from the town, went hurriedly into the nearby town of Brownsville, and wantonly shot into houses and attacked the citizens inside. This squad of soldiers, numbering, probably, not less than eight nor more than twenty, deliberately attacked and shot at citizens wherever seen in the streets and shot into many houses. They fired into hotels filled with guests and into residences occupied by men, women, and children. Their conduct indicated a wanton purpose to terrorize the inhabitants of the town and to destroy with utter reckless disregard of age, sex, or condition of helplessness. "In carrying out their unlawful purpose they respected neither the sanctity of the home nor the innocence and helplessness of women and children."[2] They fired into houses where women and children were sleeping, in some instances the bullets passing through the rooms and only a few feet over the beds in which the people were lying. One citizen was killed, one was severely wounded.

The committee majority believed the evidence supporting these facts was incontestable. Fifteen eyewitnesses testified that they saw and recognized the raiders as persons dressed in the uniform of United States soldiers, and most of these witnesses recognized them as Negroes. Two witnesses testified that they saw a number of men (one recognizing them as soldiers) on the inside of the wall of the camp, moving rapidly to the point where they went over the wall. Five witnesses testified to firing occurring inside the wall of the fort. One witness heard voices inside the wall of the camp calling to others to "Hurry up," to "Jump," and so on, and heard the men when they jumped the wall and proceeded up the alley where the firing continued. Several witnesses, who were not able to see, heard the voices of members of the attacking party and recognized them as the voices of Negroes. One witness saw a black soldier, with his gun, returning from the direction of the town where the firing had occurred, and saw him enter the reservation immediately after the shooting had stopped. Three witnesses testified as to having seen the armed men running back in the direction of the fort immediately after the shooting ceased. Others testified to having heard the raiders. The greatest distance from the fort at which any firing occurred did not exceed 350 yards, and the entire time consumed for the raid was probably not more than ten or twelve minutes.

The witnesses were described by the report as respectable and trustworthy. Their testimony alone would have been sufficient to establish beyond reasonable doubt that the shooting was done by black soldiers, and there were no black soldiers in that part of the country except those of Companies B, C, and D of the Twenty-fifth Infantry.

Other facts and circumstances corroborated the eyewitness testimony which, taken together, were conclusive of the guilt of the soldiers, said the majority report.

1) There was no evidence whatever on which to base a claim that the shooting was done by any person or persons other than by soldiers of the Twenty-fifth Infantry. "There was no class of people or individuals in that vicinity known to entertain any hostility toward the people of Brownsville."[3] There was no friction between the citizens and the police and no ill feeling among the inhabitants of the town.

2) Early in the morning of August 14, soon after the shooting, there were picked up in the streets of Brownsville, where the firing had occurred, a large number of empty shells, some loaded cartridges, clips, and one bandoleer. Of this ammunition picked up in the streets, 32 empty shells, 7 loaded cartridges, 2 or 3 clips, and 1 bandoleer were presented in evidence to the committee and identified as those manufactured for and used with the Springfield rifle used by the black battalion. A number of bullets were extracted from the houses into which they had been fired on the night of August 13-14 and were found to be substantially of the weight, size and material of those used in the Springfield rifle.

It further appeared from the marks of the four lands upon the bullets, from actual tests and other evidence, that these cartridges, with these bullets and shells in combination, could not have been fired from any other gun than the Springfield rifle, model of 1903, and that the only rifles of that kind in that section of the country were those with which the First Battalion, Twenty-fifth Infantry was armed.

It was further established, the committee report continued, from the sound of the explosions, that the firing was from high-power rifles. Many witnesses testified that the peculiar sound made by loading the guns and working the levers in extracting the empty shells during the firing was similar to that sound made by the Springfield rifle.

3) Although a majority of the committee felt that the proof was abundant and conclusive that some of the soldiers were guilty, the evidence failed to identify the particular soldier or soldiers who participated in the affray. From the nature and the character of the attack and the number of persons engaged in it, it was clearly preconcerted and probably deliberately planned and executed, the majority report asserted. It was reasonably certain that soldiers who did not actually participate in the attack must have known of it and aided those actively engaged in it in procuring their arms and ammunition and in concealing their identity when they returned.

When one considered that from ten to twenty guns had to be taken from the garrison, the report conjectured, some of them from the gun racks, supposedly locked and located near to the bunks filled with sleeping soldiers; that testimony indicated that the first firing was within the camp wall; that the firing of volley after volley by from ten to twenty men began just back of the barracks, extended into the town, and lasted from ten to twelve minutes; that the shooting began within 400 or 500 feet of a guard, with a sergeant and several privates on duty; that the participants had to return to the garrison after the firing had ceased and join their companies, then being formed; "we are forced to the conclusion that soldiers other than those who actively participated in the raid must have known of what was taking place, and were aiders and abettors thereof, either before or after the fact."[4]

The majority report was signed by the following: four of the eight Republicans — F. E. Warren, H. C. Lodge, W. Warner, and H. A. Du Pont; and all five of the Democrats — J. P. Taliaferro, Murphy J. Foster, Lee S. Overman, J. B. Frazier, and James B. McCreary.

The four Republican Senators issued, in addition, a separate statement as follows:

While the evidence has shown that the assault was perpetrated by members of the Twenty-fifth Infantry, it is reasonable to believe that not all the soldiers were concerned in the commission of the crime, either as principals or accessories.

It is true, these four Republicans continued, that in military administration the maintenance of discipline is ever a primary consideration and as a result sometimes honest and guiltless men must be subjected to injustice to the end that vicious men may be deprived of the opportunity to weaken or destroy the morale of the Army. In the present case, however, it would seem to be justice to restore to all the innocent men of these companies the rights and privileges which had accrued to them by their previous service in the Army.

These four Senators then recommended a bill the substance of which was that if within one year after the approval of that bill the President became satisfied that any former enlisted man had neither participated in nor had any knowledge of the affray he should be entitled to all the rights and privileges as of the time he was discharged.

The Minority Reports

Two minority reports were issued, the first and briefer signed by the four remaining Republicans: N. B. Scott, J. B. Foraker, J. A. Hemenway, and M. G. Bulkeley. It stated that the testimony taken was unsatisfactory, indefinite and conflicting in its nature; that while Major Penrose and other officers of the battalion at first concluded that some of the members of their companies were guilty, they later became convinced of their innocence; that a Grand Jury of the citizens of Cameron County, Texas, after investigation, was unable to indict any members of the battalion; and that many of the soldiers had served their country loyally for years.

The strongest evidence, if undisputed, implicated no greater number than from seven to twelve, and even if it were admitted for the sake of argument that this number was guilty, that fact could not justify discharging the entire battalion without honor. "The persons who were guilty of the shooting affray at Brownsville, Texas, should be severely punished – after they are proven guilty."[5]

The members issuing this minority report then offered the following conclusions:

1) The testimony failed to identify the particular individuals who participated in the shooting.

2) The testimony failed to show that the discharged soldiers entered into any agreement or so-called conspiracy of silence or that they reached any understanding to withhold information.

3) The testimony was so contradictory and much of it was so unreliable that it could not sustain the charge that any of the soldiers of the Twenty-fifth Infantry participated in the shooting affray.

4) Whereas the testimony showed that the discharged men had good records as soldiers and that many of them had by their long and faithful service acquired valuable rights of which they were then deprived; and

> Whereas the testimony showed beyond a reasonable doubt that whatever may be the fact as to who did the shooting, many of the men so discharged were innocent of any offense in connection therewith; therefore it is, in our opinion, the duty of Congress to provide by appropriate legislation for the correction of their record and for their reenlistment and reinstatement in the Army, and for the restoration to them of all the rights of which they have been deprived.

Foraker and Bulkeley, in addition to supporting the conclusions of this report, offered one of their own, a detailed brief of some eighty pages, which claimed that the weight of the testimony showed that *none* of the soldiers of the Twenty-fifth Infantry participated in the shooting.

During the spring of 1907, on March 23 and May 6, military courts-martial concluded trials of Major Penrose and Captain Edgar A. Macklin, commanding officer and officer-of-the-day respectively at the time of the raid.[6]

Major Penrose was charged with neglect of duty, with two specifications: (1) having been informed that his soldiers were guilty of the raid he failed to take the measures necessary to detect the guilty men; and (2) knowing of the feeling in the town toward the soldiers he failed to order Captain Macklin to inspect frequently the men under his command. He was found not guilty on the charge and first specification; he was found guilty of the second specification, but the court added that it did not attach any criminality to the officer's failure to give Captain Macklin more explicit orders. He was thus acquitted of any responsibility for the affray.

Captain Macklin was also charged with neglect of duty, with one specification, that he retired to his quarters from which it was found impossible to arouse him for some time. He was judged not guilty of both charge and specification. Each court, however, held that though the officers were not responsible, men of their command had committed the midnight attack.

The Case for the Soldiers

From the voluminous testimony accumulated after months of hearings, it is possible to establish an impressive case in defense of the innocence of the Brownsville soldiers.

Before the shooting incident, both the officers and the soldiers of the battalion had unblemished reputations. All of the officers of the Twenty-fifth Infantry attested to the high character of their men, their honorable fighting record, their disciplined behavior before and during their stay at Fort Brown. Almost all of the men had served more than one enlistment by August 13, 1906. Their terms of service ranged from five years to more than twenty. One enlisted man, Mingo Sanders of Company B, would have been entitled in eighteen more months to retire on three-fourths pay.

Although the townspeople of Brownsville were hardly cordial in their greeting of the black soldiers, there was no indication that the soldiers showed any resentment on account of the regulations barring them from the saloons or that in general their relations with the town residents were unusually strained. The Tate-Newton and the Baker-Reed incidents did not seem to enrage the soldiers, and as for the alleged assault upon Mrs. Evans, if there had been an assault, it would constitute a reason why the citizens might attack the soldiers, and not a reason why the soldiers should attack the citizens. In general the frame of mind in the town, even before the black soldiers arrived, suggests that the citizens were more likely to "shoot up" the soldiers than the soldiers were to "shoot up" the town.

Major Penrose testified that he was in his bed, but awake, when the first shots were fired — two shots. The two shots were followed almost immediately, he said, by six or seven more, fired rapidly. He assumed the first two shots were fired outside of the reservation. The first two were undoubtedly pistol shots, he said; the others were from high-powered guns. When questioned further he defined high-powered guns as the Springfield rifle, used in the Army, the Winchester and all the sporting rifles, including the Krag, the Savage, the Mannlicher, the Marlin and the Mauser. Captain Lyon corroborated the testimony: two pistol shots, followed by a number of shots fired from small high-caliber rifles, which might have been Government Springfields, but were not necessarily so.

A Brownsville resident, George W. Rendall, testified before the congressional committee that he thought the first shots were pistols and that he did not remember having testified more decisively earlier on this point.[7] He had, however, on August 14, the day after the shooting occurred, testified that he was sleeping and was "woke up by pistol shots fired close to my house, about 60 feet from the garrison, inside the garrison wall."[8] Later, on December 6, 1906, he testified before the Grand Jury and said:

> I was awakened by the shooting. There were two shots fired before I got up and looked out of the window. I judge they were pistol shots. The men I saw moving were inside the garrison wall, and the only shots that I saw as they left the weapons were fired upward.

Mayor Combe testified that although he could not determine whether the initial shots were fired from within the garrison or not, they did appear to him without doubt to be pistol shots.[9]

The testimony is overwhelming in pointing out that the men of the battalion had no pistols or revolvers in their possession. The only revolvers that had been issued to those companies were still in the boxes in which they had come from the arsenal. If the first shots were pistol shots, they could not have been fired by the soldiers.

There is much contradictory evidence concerning the location of the first firing. Many of the Brownsville residents testified that these first shots originated within the garrison. Two important witnesses offered contrary testimony: the sentinel on duty at the time near the point where the firing commenced, Pvt. J. H. Howard; and Matias Tamayo, a Mexican citizen of Brownsville, employed as scavenger for the reservation and working in the rear of B barracks near to the place where the first shots were fired.

Howard testified that as soon as he heard the first fusillade of firing he passed between C and B barracks to a point near the walk in front of the barracks, held his gun in the air and fired it three times, each time calling the guard for the purpose of giving alarm. He testified that there were no shots fired from within the walls of the reservation, except those three he fired.

The scavenger testified that after the first fusillade of shots he rapidly drove away in his cart; that no shots were fired from within the reservation while he was in the rear of the barracks; but that all the first shots were fired from some place outside the reservation, somewhere near the mouth of Cowen Alley.

Rendall testified that the firing awakened him; that he went at once to his window and looked out over the reservation in the direction of D barracks; that while looking he heard a shot to his left that caused him to turn and look to his left; and that he then saw two shots fired, as he thought, in the air. These were perhaps the shots fired by the sentinel. It is possible that others who claim that they saw shots fired from the barracks or from inside the reservation wall were misled in the same way.

The testimony of the officers and men alike is that the call-to-arms was sounded immediately after the first firing upon order of Major Penrose; that the men in the barracks were aroused, the gun racks were opened, and the men were formed in their respective company parade grounds. There was delay in the formation of Company C because the noncommissioned officer-in-charge-of-quarters refused to open the gun racks until he could get an order from some superior. Major Penrose ordered the gun racks broken open, and two of them were broken open by the men with axes and other implements. This company was not formed until five or ten minutes after the firing ceased, but D and B Companies were formed, or were forming, before the firing ceased. The roll of Company B was called, the call ending at about the time the firing ceased.

Captain Lyon personally inspected his men — Company D — as they fell in line, and under orders from Major Penrose placed them behind the wall of the reservation, where the roll was called and every man found to be present or accounted for. The roll call of Company C was the same. The officers were all of the opinion that while it was possible that men engaged in the firing could have rejoined their companies before verification, no one did so join. They failed to observe, as they think they would have done, if such had occurred, any excitement or quick breathing or other evidence of participation in the shooting followed by the necessarily great haste in rejoining the company.

The minority report issued by Foraker and Bulkeley, as well as the Constitution League's report before it, pointed to the assumption of guilt made by the Citizens' Committee of Brownsville and, in spite of that assumption, the indecisiveness of the eyewitness testimony. Not one of the witnesses called before the Citizens' Committee could say more than, hearing the firing, he looked out into a dark night and saw a party of men who appeared to be uniformed and armed like the soldiers from the garrison and who, on that account, were recognized as soldiers or whose speech, from some distance, was identifed as the speech of black soldiers. Both dissenting reports also stressed the inability of the Cameron County Grand Jury to indict any of the men.

Not only did Blocksom's report indicate bias on his part, but General Garlington, in his appearance before the Senate committee, frankly admitted that he had entered upon his investigation assuming that the men were guilty. His activities, he said, were directed toward discovering which of the soldiers was guilty. At no time did it occur to him that anyone other than a soldier was responsible.

The quality of his attitude toward blacks in general can be inferred from the following exchange.

> Q. Do you think colored people, generally, are truthful?
> A. (Gen E. Garlington) No, sir; I do not.
> Q. ...You would not believe their testimony ordinarily, even under oath, would you?
> A. Where their own interest or some interest was concerned. It depends entirely upon the circumstances.
> Q. You think a colored man might testify truthfully about the weather, but that he would not testify truthfully about a crime?
> A. He might have some difficulty in testifying about the weather.
> Q. Just now he would, but if he were testifying about a crime that he was charged with, or that some of his comrades were charged with, you would not believe him?
> A. Not without corroboration.[10]

The officers of the battalion originally supposed at the time of the shooting that it was done by Brownsville citizens; after being confronted with the cartridges, shells and clips they concluded that some of their men were guilty. But in the course of the investigation by the Committee on Military Affairs of the Senate, as a result of the presentation of some testimony, the officers became again convinced that the men of the battalion were innocent.

There was first of all the matter of the visibility the night of the raid. Only three of the many eyewitnesses were aided by any kind of artificial light, and the distances from which all the eyewitnesses identified the raiders as soldiers varied from 30 to 150 feet. Major Blocksom in his report, which indicted the soldiers, admitted that "Streets were poorly lighted, and it was a dark night. Those who saw them [the soldiers] were busy trying to keep out of sight themselves."[11] Captain Macklin illustrated the darkness of the night with several incidents. He had a chain of sentinels to visit regularly, and in one or two instances he could not locate the men and had to call out to them, only to discover they were no more than 10 or 15 feet away. In answer to the question as to whether he could identify the men by color at that distance, he claimed not to have been able to see anything at 15 feet. "I could not see at all. Everything was just a blank."[12] There was similar testimony from the other officers.[13]

Paulino S. Preciado testified that he was at the Tillman saloon, that he clearly saw the men who fired the volley that killed Frank Natus because of the light of the lamps that were shining in the court, that he could see distinctly how the men were armed and how they were dressed and that he recognized them positively as soldiers. He testified that the men stepped through the open gateway leading from the alley and advanced into the courtyard the distance of "two or three paces," where he could see them distinctly. This statement, however, is contradicted, first, by his own testimony given before the Grand Jury, where he stated:

Grand Jury Room, September 10, 1906
PAULINO PRECIADO, being duly sworn, deposes and says: I live in
Brownsville, Texas. On the night of the shooting, I was in the Ruby
saloon. . . the bartender went to close the door, when a volley was fired.
Natus exclaimed: "Ay Dios," and fell down; I saw him because I was
looking in that direction when the shots were fired. I saw I was in danger
and went to one side. I could not see anybody in the alley, as it was dark
out there and I was in the light. I heard no word spoken. . . . While I was
in the corner I received a slight flesh wound.[14]

The contradictory testimony so discredited the witness that it prompted
Secretary Taft to write to President Roosevelt, enclosing a copy of the
Grand Jury testimony which, in Taft's words, "contradicts and impeaches his
evidence."

Preciado's testimony is further contradicted by his statement as published two days after the shooting in his newspaper, *El Porvenir:*

> . . .The editor of *El Porvenir*. . .had just arrived at Senor Tillman's saloon
> when the shooting commenced. . . .[After the bartender was killed], the
> three gentlemen [including Preciado] sought cover in different parts of
> the house. . . .

No reference of any kind was made to Preciado's recognition of the raiders.

One explanation for his change in testimony might be found in the fact
that at the time of the last testimony he was asserting a claim against the
United States for personal injury damages he had sustained on the ground
that they were inflicted by the wrongful conduct of the soldiers. It was
necessary to his case that he establish beyond any doubt that it was the
soldiers who wounded him.

Ambrose Littlefield testified that from the mouth of Cowen Alley at
13th Street he looked 120 feet up the street to where it met Washington
Street and saw a party of raiders turning to the right from 13th Street on to
Washington Street, and that as soon as they turned into Washington Street
they passed near a street lamp, and that as they were passing the street lamp
one of the raiders turned and looked in the direction of the witness, and that
the witness, by the aid of the lamp, at that distance from him, could see that
it was the face of a black soldier.

The testimony of this witness is directly contradicted by George Thomas
Porter, who lived at the corner of 13th and Washington Streets, and who
testified that he was at his front window looking out at the very time mentioned by Littlefield, and that no men of any kind turned out of 13th Street
into Washington Street or were anywhere near the lamp under which Littlefield claimed to have seen the soldiers.

Police Lieutenant Dominguez, who was wounded, testified that from the corner of Washington and 14th Streets he looked down 14th Street to Cowen Alley and saw the raiders cross 14th Street, going northward into the alley toward the Miller Hotel. He claimed to have seen eight of the raiders, four abreast. That he could not have had any artificial light to aid him and does not pretend to have had any such help, is enough to discredit his statement.

Officer Pardon, in addition, testified that he was at the corner of Washington and 14th Streets at the time when the raiders were firing in the Cowen house, that he went from that point northward on Washington Street to 13th Street, and that when about midway in the square, he met Lieutenant Dominguez, and that Dominguez there alighted, tightened his saddle girth, remounted, and then went with Pardon north on Washington Street to 13th, and that he was never nearer 14th Street than the point where he was met, which was, as stated, in the middle of the square.

Dominguez claimed to have seen the soldiers at another time, as he was passing the mouth of the alley on 13th Street at the Miller Hotel. He testified that he passed the mouth of the alley in a fast trot, and that as he did he looked down it toward the garrison and saw at a distance of 25 or 30 feet some soldiers coming up the alley toward 13th Street. There were approximately fifteen or twenty of them, he said, and they were equally divided into two squads, were marching in single file and the squads were on opposite sides of the alley. The alley was 20 feet wide. On one side at the line of the alley rose a two-story frame building; on the opposite side at the line of the alley rose a three-story brick building, the Miller Hotel. Dominguez thus could not look into the alley until he came opposite to it. At that time he was going in a fast trot and he must have passed the mouth of the alley very rapidly.

He testified that he not only saw the soldiers and made the careful observations just noted, but that he saw a lady in the window of one of the upper stories of the hotel and was able to warn her, as well as others appearing at the hotel windows, of the danger that was approaching.

There was no light whatever in the alley, either at the point 30 feet from the mouth of it, where Dominguez claims to have seen the soldiers, or at any other point.

The eyewitness testimony contained many contradictory elements. Additional evidence to support the soldiers' claim to innocence was gathered by several experiments carried out by officers of the Twenty-fifth Infantry, none of them, though, belonging to any of the companies stationed at Brownsville.[15] Second Lieutenant James Blyth testified that at Fort McIntosh, during February and March, 1907, two kinds of experiments were carried out, some with respect to the power of vision at night and some with respect to the course of bullets. The observers included, in addtion to himself, Major O'Neil, Lieutenant Harbold, Lieutenant Elser, and a civilian by the name of Colonel Stucke who was simply a dinner guest of Major O'Neil's. The experiments were conducted by Lieutenant Wiegenstein. He told the men involved nothing at all about the experiment, but at about eight in the evening the officers were led to the edge of an arroyo. There were men already placed at the bottom of it. A volley was fired and Major O'Neil shouted and asked which way the men were facing. None of the observers could tell. Lieutenant Wiegenstein laughed and said that was a part of the test, that he wanted the observers to discover for themselves. The observers then moved down about 50 feet further along the edges of the arroyo. Two more volleys were fired, but all the observers claimed they could see was the flash of the rifle. They could not even see the rifle that fired the bullets.

That first firing was at a distance of 50 feet and 4 inches horizontally and 21 feet and 2 inches vertically. At that distance the observers could not distinguish the men, their clothing, or even the direction from which they were firing. A second firing took place, at a different distance, comparable to a different set of details from the night of the raid, but the results were the same.

During another test the observers moved 69 feet away from and 20 feet above the men. Looking almost into their faces when the volleys were fired, all they could see, they testified, was the flash. Indeed, the closer the observers got to the source of the firing, the more the flash of the rifle blinded them.

Later that night the men were brought up on the bank to the road which was about 8 feet wide. The observers were divided into two groups, one group placed on either side of the road. The moon was shining, and it was a clear starlit night. The men were marched in single file, between the two groups of observers. After they all passed one witness said that he asked Major O'Neil to have a number of white officers march by so that he might have a varied sample. Lieutenant Wiegenstein then informed him that there had been white men in the original line. The detail was then halted and the observers went to within two feet of the men. "I peered right into their faces," said one of the observers, "and I myself picked out one man who was a little lighter colored than the remainder, and he turned out to be a Mexican. The others I could not distinguish at all. After we had passed he told me that there was a white man in the center of the line."[16]

Later that night the party went out again, after the moon was down, and the results were substantially the same.

Some weeks later another set of experiments was held. Similar tests were held in the arroyo, with similar results. Then the men were moved around in front of a house in which the witnesses were sitting, and marched around the parade ground, with a light behind them. When they got some 60 feet away the observers testified that they disappeared entirely from view. The men were brought back and marched between a street lamp and the house, a distance of about 20 paces. The observers were unable to recognize anyone. Then the men were brought around on the sidewalk right in front of the house, just 5 paces away. At that distance the observers failed to recognize Lieutenant Wiegenstein, who was in the center.

Several of the participants testified to the significance of the experiments: that even on a bright night, and under conditions simulating or better than those described as existing the night of the raid, the observers could not distinguish the color of the men or the clothing they were wearing.

Other experiments tested the assertion by Major Blocksom and others that the course of certain bullets after they struck the houses into which they were shot indicated that they were fired from the upper porch of B barracks. Lieutenant Harbold testified to experiments he conducted with the Krag-Jorgensen rifle, the Springfield rifle and the Winchester rifle to get the penetration and deflection of different bullets from those rifles. He found that it was a general rule that all bullets were deflected after passing through a first object, but that the rule of deflection could not be determined. It was irregular, he said, sometimes to the right, then to the left, another time upward and still again downward. The only general rule he could ascertain was that the bullets would be deflected in some way.[17] The deflection apparently depended upon the direction in which the point or nose of the bullet happened to be turned when it struck the obstruction and on the density of the material. He set up targets to simulate the walls of the homes in Brownsville, and concluded from the firings into those targets that the deflections were so irregular that it was not possible to reach an accurate judgment, based upon the bullet holes in several walls, concerning the source of the firing.

In the course of the courts-martial of the officers and the investigation before the Senate committee, evidence of the shells, clips and cartridges, by which the officers had first been led to think their men guilty, was reexamined and became the proof to them that their men were, as they had originally believed, innocent of the shooting.

According to the weight of the testimony there were from 150 to 200 shots fired that night in Brownsville by the raiders, whoever they may have been. Although careful search was made, only forty shells were discovered. Seven of these empty shells were found by Captain Macklin at the mouth of Cowen Alley near the fort. Thirty-three others were found in the alley and in Washington Street where the firing was said to have occurred, and these were turned over to the authorities and ultimately to the Senate for use as evidence. None of the remaining shells were discovered or at least submitted.

Captain Macklin, who was the officer of the day, testified that just at the break of dawn, he made a careful search for any evidence that would help identify the guilty parties. He searched both inside and outside the reservation wall to discover shells, clips or any other incriminating evidence, to test the citizens' claims that the soldiers were the raiders. He found no evidence inside the fort. Outside the wall, across the street, where, according to the testimony of the guard, the scavenger, and other witnesses, the first shots were heard, he found seven shells and six clips in a circular area not more than 10 inches in diameter. Army experts testified that if these shells had fallen from Springfield rifles as they were fired, they would have been scattered over an area perhaps 10 feet in diameter. It was the opinion of all the witnesses who testified on that point that the shells found by Captain Macklin could not have fallen in the position in which he found them. This bit of evidence, coupled with the further realization that with these seven shells were found six clips, enough to hold thirty cartridges, further discredited the discovery of the shells as establishing the soldiers' guilt.

The War Department seized all the rifles that belonged to the three companies and sent them to the Springfield Armory, where they were fired and their cartridges examined microscopically. That is, the indentations on the heads of the exploded shells were compared with the indentations found on the heads of the thirty-three exploded shells found in the streets of Brownsville.[18] The results of the report indicated:

1) There was such an exact identity between the indentations on the thirty-three exploded shells and the indentations found upon shells exploded from four guns belonging to Company B of the Twenty-fifth Infantry that the examiners reported that beyond any doubt the shells picked up in the streets of Brownsville had been fired from those four guns.

2) The experts found that three of these shells had a double indentation, as though a first attempt to fire them had failed and they had then been put into the gun a second time and struck a second time with the hammer or firing pin before they were exploded.

3) They further reported that nine of the shells bore marks indicating that they had twice or oftener been inserted in a rifle as though to be fired.

How can a case defending the innocence of the soldiers exploit this War Department report?

On the question of the double indentation, many officers and men testified that when they first received their rifles, some time during the end of April, 1906, at Fort Niobrara, they were found to be so heavily oiled with cosmoline that the spring which shot the bolt forward with the firing pin to strike the head of the cartridge and explode it was impeded to such an extent that frequently the cartridges failed to explode at the first stroke. But after that, by the use of coal oil and in other ways, the cosmoline had been entirely removed so that the spring worked freely. The witnesses examined on this point all testified that long before the troops left Fort Niobrara, where they used their rifles in target practice, they stopped having any such difficulty.

As to the double insertion of cartridges, the officers and men questioned on this point testified that while they were engaged in target practice at Fort Niobrara the call to cease fire was often sounded after a cartridge had been inserted but before it was fired. At that point the soldier was required to remove at once any cartridge from his gun. This cartridge was later reinserted and fired when firing was resumed. In this way shells would show marks indicating that they had been inserted more than once. The officers and men testified that except on the target range at Fort Niobrara, there was never any such double insertion of cartridges or any occasion for such double insertion.

The officers' testimony illustrated how improbable it was that such a double insertion would have occurred during the shooting affray at Brownsville. When an attempt is made to fire a cartridge and the attempt fails, the bolt must be drawn back, with the result that the ejector throws the cartridge out of the chamber and to a distance of anywhere from 3 to 10 feet from the gun. The idea that a raider would undertake during a raid and in the darkness to recover an ejected cartridge is utterly untenable. The same argument holds for the double indentation.

The four guns which fired the shells located in Brownsville were identified by their numbers. On the night of the shooting three of these guns were assigned to Thomas Taylor, Joseph L. Wilson and Ernest English, all privates of Company B. These men testified that they were in their quarters asleep when the firing began, that they heard the call-to-arms, rushed with their comrades to the gun racks, each receiving some gun which he carried for that night and which he returned to the gun racks after the company was dismissed for the night, where they were locked up until morning. The following morning each soldier located his own gun in the gun rack, and when submitted for inspection, all guns were found to be clean, providing no evidence whatever of having been fired the night before. All testified that in the excitement and confusion each soldier grabbed the first gun he could get but that all the guns were found in the racks where they were verified after the firing ceased.

Lieutenant Lawrason testified that he heard for the first time that his soldiers were accused of the firing when Mayor Combe appeared. He had, he said, already accounted for all of the rifles and for all of the men, including the three mentioned, that although he did not see them they answered the roll call, and that he was familiar enough with the voice of each man in his company to detect any irregularity.[19]

The testimony indicated that the fourth gun could not have been fired that night. It was originally issued at Fort Niobrara to Sergeant Blaney. Shortly before the battalion left Fort Niobrara for Brownsville his term of enlistment expired. He reenlisted and took the usual furlough of three months to which he was entitled. Before starting his furlough he turned his gun in to the quartermaster-sergeant, Walker McCurdy, who wrote his name on a piece of paper, placed it with the gun in the arms chest and locked it. Sergeant Blaney did not return to the company until after it left Fort Brown. On the night of the shooting his gun, with others, was still in this arms chest. All such guns were placed there when the battalion left Fort Niobrara. On arrival at Fort Brown the arms chest was put in the store room, and for want of space, other baggage was piled on top of the chest.

On the night of the firing, and immediately after the company was dismissed for the night, Lieutenant Lawrason, the company commander, under orders from Major Penrose, proceeded to verify his rifles. He carefully counted the rifles in the gun racks and found there the exact number that belonged in the racks. Sometime later he went to the storeroom, taking with him the quartermaster-sergeant, who unlocked the room. He told the quartermaster-sergeant that he wished to verify the guns in his custody — those in the arms chest. The quartermaster-sergeant thereupon removed the baggage that had been piled on top of the arms chest, unscrewed the lid, and exposed the guns. Lieutenant Lawrason counted them and found that every gun was there. In this way he established that Blaney's gun was at the time of the firing in the arms chest and that the door of the storeroom was fastened under lock and key. In other words, it appears impossible for that gun to have been fired in Brownsville.

Quartermaster-Sergeant Walker McCurdy testified[20] that Sergeant Blaney's rifle, number 45683, was placed in the arms chest by him with Blaney's name placed on top of it to prevent it from being issued to anyone else, and that it was not issued again except to Blaney after the shooting, that during the entire time the companies were in Fort Brown that rifle was locked in the chest, covered with oil, with a slip of paper identifying it as Blaney's on top of it, in a chest on top of which was piled excess baggage.

If this gun, then, was not fired that night in Brownsville, as the testimony concluded, then it follows that if the shells picked up in the streets of Brownsville were fired out of this gun, they must have been fired at Fort Niobrara.

Before the microscopic inspection was made or any such question foreseen, it was established by uncontradicted testimony that Company B took with it to Brownsville as part of its baggage a box containing from 1,600 to 2,000 exploded shells with a proportionate number of clips, and that after arriving at Brownsville this box stood open on the back porch of B barracks, where anyone passing might have access to it and remove shells and clips from it.

The microscopic report said that the shells picked up from the streets of Brownsville were fired out of four guns of B Company. If so, then it also follows that they were fired, not in Brownsville, but at Fort Niobrara, and that they were found in the streets, not because they fell there when fired, but because they had been placed there by persons unknown, who had secured them from the box of shells standing on the back porch where they were easily accessible to anyone disposed to remove them. The microscopic inspection showed, not that the soldiers were guilty of the firing, but that the soldiers were free from such guilt.

The microscopic inspection did not establish anything more than that the shells found were fired from the four guns mentioned. It did not indicate the time or place when they were fired or the parties who fired them. General Crozier, Chief of Ordnance, concluded his review of the testimony as follows:

> The bearing of these facts upon the identity of the persons doing the firing and upon the time when the cases and bullets were fired in the guns is not a concern of this department.[21]

A bandoleer, such as soldiers used, was discovered in Cowen Alley the morning after the firing. It was placed in evidence against the soldiers. Each of the quartermaster-sergeants of the three companies testified that before the men left Fort Niobrara every bandoleer was returned to the arsenal; that no bandoleer was issued from the time of their arrival at Brownsville until the companies were formed after the shooting began; that consequently the bandoleer that was found could not have belonged to any soldiers of the Twenty-fifth Infantry. The testimony further showed that when the Twenty-sixth Infantry left Fort Brown, a few days before the arrival of the Twenty-fifth Infantry, the men left some bandoleers in the barracks. These were carried away by scavengers and citizens of Brownsville, along with articles of discarded clothing and other articles left behind. In addition, there would be no reason why the soldiers, if they planned the raid as is claimed, should carry a bandoleer and throw it away in the street when they could carry many times more cartridges than they had any need for in their regular belts.

Seven bullets and parts of the steel jackets of two other bullets were cut from houses into which it is claimed they were fired that night. These bullets bore the marks of four lands, such as would be made by a Springfield rifle, which the soldiers had, or a Krag rifle or a Krag carbine or a Mauser rifle. They must have been fired from a Springfield rifle, it was claimed, because the exploded shells that were found in the street indicated that the bullets belonged to Springfield rifle cartridges.

It was further claimed that these cartridges were too long to have been fired from the Krag rifle or carbine. But the bullets that were cut out of the houses could not be identified as coming from a Springfield rifle or a Krag rifle or a Krag carbine. The Springfield and Krag bullets are of the same weight and the same general appearance. Many witnesses testified that it was impossible to judge from the bullets what kind of rifle had been used.

Even if the bullets were fired out of the shells that were picked up in the streets it does not necessarily mean that the rifles from which they were fired were Springfield rifles, for the testimony showed that by slightly reaming out the bore of the Krag rifle, the Springfield cartridge could be inserted in it and fired from it.

There was also evidence that at least four Krag rifles were disposed of to citizens of Brownsville by the quartermaster-sergeant of Company K of the Twenty-sixth Infantry shortly before the arrival of the Twenty-fifth Infantry.

There was further indication that other Krag rifles were in the possession of Brownsville residents. Mayor Combe testified that the Texas Rangers were formerly armed with the Krag carbine, out of which Springfield cartridges could have been fired if the bores were reamed.

A number of bullets taken from the houses of Brownsville citizens were found by chemical analysis to correspond in composition to a special lot of bullets manufactured and supplied to the Government by the Union Metallic Cartridge Company under a contract dated June 29, 1905.

The testimony showed that the black troops were supplied in part with cartridges from this lot, but it also showed that the companies of the Twenty-sixth Infantry stationed previously at Fort Brown were supplied with the same kind of ammunition and that when they left Fort Brown a few days before the arrival of the Negro troops they left many of these cartridges scattered about the barracks. Citizens were allowed to and did visit the barracks and carry them away at pleasure.[22] The ammunition of the Twenty-fifth Infantry, on the other hand, had been accounted for almost to the cartridge.

Such was the essence of the case defending the Brownsville soldiers against the accusation that some of their number had carried out the raid the night of August 13.

The Foraker minority report added a somewhat gratuitous defense: ". . .the formation and execution of such a conspiracy would require a higher order of ability than any of the men of the battalion possessed."[23] Certainly any men capable of planning such a raid, the report went on, and so managing its execution as to defy detection, would not be so foolish as to begin operations by firing from their own quarters and grounds, and then, after having thus aroused the town and fixed their identity as soldiers, jump over the wall and start their activities.

The dissenting report stressed the inadequate motive offered as explanation for the soldiers' raid. It had been said that the raiders fired into Starck's house, mistaking it for Tate's house, which it adjoined, and that Tate was the intended victim because of the wrongs he had done to Newton. But some months prior to the affray, Starck, who was a customs officer, had undertaken to arrest a smuggler by the name of Avillo, who lived in Brownsville and who had worked for Starck. Avillo resisted arrest and Starck struck him to the ground with his revolver. Avillo was put under bond to appear in court but forfeited his bond, and was at the time of the shooting a fugitive from justice. It is likely, the report concluded, that the men who shot into Starck's house knew precisely whose house they were attacking. Starck himself had referred to the more than 600 arrests of smugglers for which he had been responsible. As for Dominguez' injury, it was more likely to have been caused by some of the numerous criminals he had arrested during his long service as municipal officer, claimed the minority report, than by soldiers with no grievances.

The case for the soldiers was impressive. How did the Government respond?

NOTES

1. From the *Brownsville Herald*, Brownsville, Texas, August 22, 1906.
2. *Report of the Senate Committee on Military Affairs*, p. 2.
3. *Ibid.*, p. 3.
4. *Ibid.*, p. 4.
5. *Ibid.*, p. 5.
6. Records of the two trials are found in U.S. Senate, 60th Cong., 1st sess., Doc. 402, pt. 2, Vol. XX, ser. no. 5253 *Proceedings of a General Court-Martial . . . in the Case of Major Charles W. Penrose* and in U.S. Senate, 60th Cong., 1st sess., Doc. 402, pt. 3, Vol XXI, ser. no. 5254 *Proceedings of a General Court-Martial . . . in the Case of Captain Edgar A. Macklin.*
7. *Report of Senate Committee on Military Affairs*, pp. 2039-40.
8. *Ibid.*, pp. 75-76
9. *Ibid.*, pp. 2383, 2423, 2440.
10. *Ibid.*, p. 2746.
11. *Ibid.*, p. 63.
12. *Ibid.*, p. 3127.
13. *Ibid.*, pp. 3146, 1735, 3154.
14. *Ibid.*, p. 2341.
15. *Ibid.*, pp. 1989 ff.
16. *Ibid.*, p. 3025.
17. *Ibid.*, pp. 1870 ff.
18. *Ibid.*, pp. 1309-25.
19. *Ibid.*, pp. 1579-80.
20. *Ibid.*, p. 1658.
21. *Ibid.*, p. 36.
22. See especially the testimony of Quartermaster-Sergeant Row, *ibid.*, p. 2317.
23. *Ibid.*, p. 75.

IV

THE GOVERNMENT ANSWERS

Yes, sir, I am a victim of that Brownsville episode,
Where Herod was outdistanced by a civil unjust code,
And this is the bit of paper that says I was not true
Against my unsullied army life, the years I wore the blue.

Why, sir, I fought the redskins in the Garden of the Gods,
When we gambled with eternity and death had heavy odds.
I climbed old San Juan Hill when the "Riders" cheeks were pale,
When the world was shown that color could face the leaden bail.

I campaigned in the Islands where nature vied with man
To murder U.S. soldiers with an alapathic plan;
See here my service striped with a record without flaw,
My life was an edition of the regulation law.

But what of that and what of this and all that I had done,
They ordered me one night to stand on guard Post No. One.
In a Texas town of my own land, in the nation of the free,
With men created equal by the code of liberty.

And on that night, it was supposed, a few revengeful blacks
From among the guards off duty, with guns outside the racks,

53

Stole out the barracks unbeknown, save those within the plot,
And made the streets of Brownsville, somehow, extremely hot.

I fired my gun and roused the camp, not knowing what it meant,
And stayed there at my station, until relief was sent.
I did my faithful duty until the row was past;
I did not know a thing about the firing, first to last.

And because I did that duty, fearless of friend or foe,
And would not swear out falsely to things I could not know,
I was kicked out of the army "without honor" in disgrace,
A byword of derision to the service and my race.

Yes, sir, I am a victim of that Brownsville episode,
Where Herod was outdistanced by a civil unjust code,
But the honor of a soldier can not be brushed away
By some Sivaltic order within this age and day.

Sherman D. Richardson[1]

Major Blocksom submitted three different statements in answer to charges against him. In all of them he defended his original report. A compilation of the three statements would appear something as follows:

I did not rely upon the evidence taken before the Citizens' Committee in Brownsville. Naturally, such a committee would be prejudiced. It was, however, composed of the best people in town, and I was informed that the majority were originally Northern men. I relied primarily upon my own investigation of the witnesses to the shooting. I interrogated some 50 witnesses who either personally saw the soldiers do the shooting or heard their voices or were witnesses to some other important aspect of the crime. I had long conversations with many other persons, and I did not hear a single person express a doubt on the subject.

The claim by the defenders of the soldiers that every man at the roll call of the three companies was present or accounted for within five to eight minutes of the first firing and that the alarm was coincident with the first firing is untrue. Also, as I have said many times, I never believed the first roll calls were accurate. Officers and the first sergeants thought the post was being attacked by the townspeople, and it is absurd to suppose they thought of roll calls first and defense afterwards.

With regard to the call-to-arms, it did not occur until several minutes after the first shots were fired, and then by order of the sergeant-of-the-guard. I believe he sounded it to create confusion, to get out and place arms in the hands of all men so that the raiders would not be discovered on their return.

If the raiders were attempting to attack the fort, not a single shot struck anything or anybody in the post. No rifles were examined for cleanliness before morning. The raiders probably all got back before the line of defense was formed. If any were late it would have been easy to slip in during the confusion.

Many officers and men claim that the time elapsed from the call-to-arms to the calling of the roll was about eight minutes. Then at least ten or eleven minutes would have lapsed between the first shots and the roll calls. I think all the evidence indicates it was longer. In any case, the raiders were in a great hurry and could easily have made the raid in ten or eleven minutes, as it is about 350 yards from the barrack wall to Tillman's saloon, the farthest point.

As to cartridges, clips and bandoleers found in the streets, they were merely corroborative evidence.

Exception is taken to my statement "It must be confessed the colored soldier is much more aggressive on the social equality question than he used to be." But I believe that the question of equality does enter as a fundamental cause of the racial antagonism existing between the Fort Brown soldiers and the residents of the town.

I did not start with the assumption that the soldiers were guilty. I had and have no prejudice against colored men. I have served with them in garrison and in the field and have often seen them under fire. When properly led there are no better soldiers. The Brownsville case arose from causes external to ordinary discipline. Racial differences may cause many such incidents to arise in the future if not checked.

Blocksom's defense of his investigation, which scored some telling points, did not touch upon much of the rest of the case put together by the defenders of the Brownsville soldiers. But the government in other reports offered substantial explanations for many of the remaining accusations and charges.

The expert evidence submitted to the Senate committee identifying certain cartridge shells picked up in Cowen Alley after the raid as having been fired from guns issued to members of Company B is conclusive. The sole flaw seems to be in the identification of one of the guns issued to Private Blaney and supposed to have been locked up in an arms chest in the storeroom of B barracks. The records of guns issued were kept by the quartermaster-sergeant and showed numerous changes and irregularities. There was no actual inspection of the guns in the arms chest until long after the raid. It was known and acknowledged that guns were being changed more or less among the men without authority. If the Blaney gun was out, there was ample opportunity to return it without detection. In general the discipline and rigor of routine was something less than desirable.

The argument advanced in defense of the soldiers that these shells came from a box of empty shells lying open on the gallery of B barracks, that they had been taken by the townspeople and scattered to throw suspicion on the soldiers, was buttressed by the further explanation that several of them showed double firing marks, due to a failure of the first attempt, the firing mechanism being heavy with cosmoline on the weapons when issued. These shells had come from the target range at Fort Niobrara, it was claimed. The argument is challenged by two facts:

1) The box mentioned contained more than a thousand shells discharged from nearly fifty rifles, thrown in indiscriminately and roughly shaken in the transportation and numerous handlings. There would be statistically only one chance in hundreds of millions that out of this box thirty shells selected at random would exhibit the absolute firing marks of only three rifles out of nearly fifty.

2) Six of the thirty shells showed marks of having been inserted in a rifle twice. No such proportion of misfires — one in five, or 20 per cent — was reported from Fort Niobrara, was in evidence on the remainder of the shells, or was claimed by the soldiers to whom the guns identified with the shells were issued.

But the conclusive evidence as to the double markings on these shells came from former Assistant Attorney-General Purdy, who explained that several of the shells picked up at Brownsville were in his presence inserted in a Springfield rifle and tested by an army officer at Fort Sam Houston to illustrate the working of the guns. Purdy thus explained the double markings. Moreover, in case two attempts were made to fire a cartridge, the primer markings of the first and unsuccessful attempt would be completely obliterated by the great or explosive blow of the second and successful attempt.

Lieutenant Lawrason originally estimated that from one-fourth to one-third of Company B came to roll call at the time of the raid without ammunition. Before the Senate committee he raised his estimate to one-half. The resulting confusion, when the men had to be sent back for their ammunition, was evidently part of a premeditated plan to secure as much delay as possible in calling the roll to enable the raiders sufficient time to return to formation. From eight to ten minutes elapsed before the roll call was under way; the raiders had by then returned. The entire distance covered by the raiders from the fort to the Tillman saloon, the farthest point, and back, could be and was covered in less than six minutes from the firing of the first shot. A fast walk out and a run back would do it in less than three minutes by actual test. The distance is less than one-sixth of a mile each way. Allow a speed of a mile in twelve minutes there and of a mile in six minutes back, and the entire distance could be covered in three minutes. Allow a minute for delays in firing, and the raid could be accomplished in four minutes. It was indeed carefully planned and well-timed.

There was a good deal of confusion in the testimony as to the use of revolvers by one or more of the raiders. Although no evidence had been obtained that service revolvers had been surreptitiously taken, it was well known that at Fort Niobrara a search had been made and several revolvers collected from members of the battalion. Testimony as to the sound of pistol shots was, under the circumstances, not conclusive or of great importance.

The most curious aspect of the Government's handling of the Brownsville affair concerns the role of Herbert J. Browne. President Roosevelt, caught between his commitment to the order dismissing the soldiers and Foraker's unsettling defense of them, hired Browne and the head of a Negro detective agency in Richmond, William B. Baldwin, to circulate among the then-dispersed ex-soldiers and ferret out the guilty men. Browne and Baldwin, in April, 1908, with what they described as "a large force of detectives," sought out and interviewed many of the former soldiers of the Twenty-fifth. The men were again engaged in September and December of 1908. In their report of December 5, 1908,[2] submitted to General George B. Davis, Judge Advocate General of the War Department, they presented a confession from former Private Boyd Conyers, formerly of B Company, who admitted his participation in the raid and discussed the planning of the raid and the other conspirators.

In submitting the confession of Boyd Conyers, Browne admitted that there were discrepancies in Conyers' many statements but he described them as of a minor character, and he attributed them to the fact that the detective who heard most of the confession, William Lawson, was illiterate and had to rely on his memory. Lawson was unacquainted with the details of the Brownsville raid and was able to provide information to his employer, Baldwin, which could have come only from one familiar with the secret history of the affair. This information was supposed to have been obtained at different times during the month of June, 1908.

Lawson's first report included the names of Conyers, John Holloman, John Brown and "another man." Subsequently he supplied the name of James Powell, and later, other names. This information was, according to Browne's report, corroborated in the presence of witnesses, but before Lawson could finish his work, Conyers became suspicious and would give no further information incriminating himself. From then on he furnished to A. H. Baldwin, Captain W. C. Baldwin and Browne information piecemeal and reluctantly.

According to Browne's report, Conyers tried to commit suicide after he discovered that he had made his statements to a detective, declaring that some of the former soldiers would kill him. He finally wrote to Foraker and received a reply. The reply he construed to mean, according to Browne, that he should stick to his original story told before the Senate committee, that he had no information, and that is what he did.

Foraker's letter, which Browne claimed Conyers construed to mean that

Foraker wanted Conyers to return to his original story, a lie, read in full:

On my return here I found awaiting me your letter of July 24th. I hardly know from what you state what it is that has transpired nor do I know just what it is I should do to get the character of information to which you refer. If you will write me again at your convenience, giving me a clearer account I will be glad to avail myself of it to the extent it may be useful. I remember you very well as a witness before the Committee and I am sure you did not there testify to anything except only the truth.

How the original, along with several photostats, ended up in the War Department file is perplexing, unless Conyers volunteered it.

Browne commented that he had "every reason to believe that Conyers' confession is genuine and gives for the first time the true secret history of the Brownsville raid." But with the influences shown to be pressing Conyers to adhere to his earlier false testimony given before the Senate Committee, Browne went on, he cannot be relied upon to support his own confession until it is thoroughly sustained from other sources.

The investigation, Browne reported, had been conducted with strict recognition of the advisability of preserving secrecy and with discretion. No promises of immunity were made.

Browne's report then offered a narrative version of Conyers' confession. A summary of Conyers' confession follows.

Conyers' Confession

When rumors of trouble over the assignment of black troops to Brownsville were circulated before the troops left Fort Niobrara, preparations were made by the men to "get even with the crackers," and so some cartridges were held out at range practice and more along the route to Brownsville. Lieutenant Lawrason of Company B threatened punishment to the men who were short of ammunition but nothing was done about it.

The friction with citizens of Brownsville began at once. In Conyers' words, "Whiskey made all the trouble. If we hadn't been drinking we wouldn't have had the nerve to shoot up the town."

At a meeting August 13 in Allison's saloon a few men agreed that the raid should take place that night at midnight. John Holloman, the money lender of Company B, was the chief conspirator and leader, but his plans could not have been carried out had not Sergeant George Jackson of Company B, in charge of the keys of the gun racks in B barracks, and Sergeant Reid, in command of the guards, cooperated both before and after the raid.

The four men who led the raid were John Holloman, John Brown, Carolina de Saussure, and himself, Boyd Conyers, all of Company B, and probably R. C. Collier, of Company C. Holloman organized the raiders. He was in the barracks, Brown was in the bake shop. Conyers and de Saussure slept in the same bunk in the guardhouse, claiming that they wanted to get under the mosquito net. They had the trick of taking their guns into the bunk instead of placing them in the open rack, on the excuse that they didn't rust so badly under cover, but really so the absence of the guns from the open guardhouse rack would not attract attention and their own absence would be ascribed to a visit to the toilet, which was back of the guardhouse. These two men slipped out the rear door of the guardhouse to join Holloman and Brown.

The party crossed the wall of the fort down near the end of A barracks, went up the roadway to the entrance of Cowen Alley, where the signal shots were fired. These shots were immediately tallied onto by the alarm shots of Joseph B. Howard, guard on No. 2, and formed the series testified to by Mrs. Leahy of Brownsville. Her testimony is further borne out by the statement that not more than thirty seconds elapsed before a number of men of Company B swarmed out on the upper gallery and opened fire on the town.

It would have been impossible for Sergeant Jackson to have opened the gun racks, for the men to have assembled, secured their guns, loaded them, gone out to the gallery, and started firing, all after the first shot was fired, all aroused, as they testified unanimously, from sound slumber, in less than two minutes, in the confusion of a dark barracks room. The racks had been opened and the inside conspirators were ready to pour out on the signal shots. There were scarcely twenty seconds between the last of the signal shots and the first general volley from B barracks. Less than five minutes elapsed from the time the first shot was fired until these men were all back inside the fort.

The number firing from the barracks is unknown, but perhaps twenty men were involved. A smaller number followed the leaders up the alley.

When Conyers and de Saussure reached the guardhouse they ran in the back way and got into their bunks. Sergeant Reid came in and swore at them, but Conyers was so excited and out of breath that he could hardly stand, so Sergeant Reid stationed him at the rear of the guardhouse in the dark where he could not be closely scrutinized. Earlier Conyers had told Sergeant Reid that they were going to shoot up the town and he laughed and said: "Don't go out there and let the crackers get the best of you." After the raid was completed Holloman came around with extra cartridges and Reid passed them out. The guns were all easily cleaned before daylight.

Such is the substance of Conyers' confession according to the affidavit of William Lawson.

Lawson (who had to sign with a mark) swore that he received this information from Boyd Conyers on several different occasions in June, 1908. Browne also swore that he received similar information from Boyd Conyers in order to corroborate the signed statement of Lawson. Browne claimed that the original declaration to Lawson was that of a criminal boasting to one of his race of his crime and of his success in escaping discovery. But his subsequent declarations to him were given partly during moments of contrition and partly as the result of careful and peristent questioning.

Browne's report claimed that there was also strong circumstantial evidence implicating Private R. L. Collier in the raid as well as several of the guard relief with knowledge after the raid.

After Sergeant Reid gave noncommittal testimony to Major A. P. Blocksom and was discharged without honor with the rest of the battalion, he disappeared, according to Browne. His testimony was never taken at any of the subsequent courts-martial and investigations. Efforts to locate him were unsuccessful. "He is constantly on the move and acts like a fugitive from justice."

John Holloman, according to the report, the chief conspirator and organizer of the raid is "an interesting character." He was serving his fourth enlistment and had been previously discharged with "character good," "character excellent," and "character very good." His reputation among his fellow soldiers, however, did not bear out his official record. He was said to be the offspring of a small Jewish trader and a mulatto woman in Georgia. Perhaps understandably he held the position as "battalion Shylock." He was not only a money lender, charging at least 20 per cent interest, but he was a successful gambler and card sharp. Half the battalion owed him money. Even the impeccable first sergeant, Mingo Sanders, was in his debt at the time of the raid. Holloman was also the financial backer and half-owner of the Allison saloon.

"Perhaps the most singular omission in the record of the raid is in his case," Browne said. John Holloman's testimony was never taken at Brownsville or anywhere else by army officers, Government officials or the Constitution League. He did not appear at the Macklin or Penrose courts-martial or before the Senate committee. After his discharge he traveled briefly with Sergeant Reid. He soon settled in Macon, Georgia, where he purchased a small grocery store.

It had been comparatively easy to trace the location of the former members of Companies C and D, the report said, but extremely difficult to find the men of Company B, especially the suspects named by Conyers.

The published testimony of the noncommissioned officers on post, Browne asserts, indicated that they were embarrassed by conflicting purposes — to satisfy the inquiries being made and yet not betray the guilty men. Browne presented testimony from several different hearings and investigations from the several men who were in the vicinity of the guardhouse, on sentinel and guard duty, and in most cases the men were vague, uncertain and uncommunicative. For example, Private J. B. Howard of Company D, sentinel on Post No. 2, "demonstrated how much he could say and how little he could tell in four examinations – at Brownsville, at the Macklin and Penrose courts-martial and before the Senate Committee."

The circumstances of the firing from B barracks, from the ground inside the wall, and the general comment which must have ensued among the men, the Browne report went on, made absurd any theory that the members of the battalion in barracks B, C, and D could have failed to have known that soldiers did the shooting. The general resentment among them at the hostile attitude of the citizens of Brownsville was sufficient to initiate the conspiracy of silence. In addition, a murder was committed and the state of Texas was involved in seeking to punish the criminals.

The discharge of the whole battalion, salutary and necessary as it was, made out of the issue a racial confrontation. Had the battalion been composed of white soldiers instead of colored, "no maudlin sympathy would have been aroused over its discharge without honor and the whole affair would have blown over in a month," Browne's report concluded.

The entire episode surrounding the detectives remains murky. In a highly dramatic and effective speech on the floor of the Senate, Foraker produced an affidavit from Boyd Conyers denying the entire series of claims by William Lawson, asserting that he never at any time spoke privately with him at all, that Sheriff E. C. Arnold was present at all of the interviews between Browne and himself and knew that Conyers consistently denied any knowledge of the raid, made no confession, and that Herbert Browne's report, published in the *Congressional Record* of December 14, was a misrepresentation of the truth.

Foraker bolstered his case by submitting an affidavit from E. C. Arnold, Sheriff of Walton County, Georgia. Arnold claimed in the affidavit that he and Browne put Conyers through the "most rigid examination I have ever seen any person subjected to in all my long experience in dealing with criminals. I have always believed that some of the soldiers 'shot up Browns-ville,' and for this reason I was glad of an opportunity to aid in getting at the bottom of it." He claimed that he was present at both of the very long interviews Browne had with Conyers, assisting Browne in every way possible. Browne claimed he was corroborating a confession Conyers had made to Lawson, that he was direct from the President and "was prepared to offer Conyers absolute immunity from any punishment and a pardon from the President if he would only tell what he knew. . . .We made all sorts of promises to him; then we told him what the consequences would be if he did not tell it, but he still denied knowing anything or who did the shooting." Browne advised him that he knew of his previous confession to Lawson. Conyers said Lawson had lied; that he had had no talk with him about the matter at all. Browne told him that some twenty soldiers had already admitted guilt and if he wanted to escape punishment he had better admit it too. Conyers still denied knowing anything. "The report of Mr. Herbert J. Browne in this matter as published in the *Congressional Record* of December 14, in so far as it related to these conversations with Boyd Conyers, is not true. To the contrary, and I say it under my solemn oath, it is the most absolutely false, the most willful misrepresentation of the truth, and the most shameful perversion of what really did take place between them that I have ever seen over the signature of any person." So spoke the Sheriff.

How did Browne come up with the names he did? Arnold claimed that when Browne utterly failed to get any information out of Conyers, he asked him to give him the names of some of the baseball players and also the names of some of the most reckless and turbulent members of his company. This Conyers did, giving several names, and these same names, so given by Conyers, Browne, in his report, says were furnished him by Conyers as the ones participating in the shooting.

Foraker submitted another affidavit from Frederick D. McGarity, assistant cashier of the leading bank in Monroe, Georgia. He said, under oath, that a gentleman who introduced himself as A. H. Baldwin, learning that he was a notary public, asked him to go with him to the house of one Lewis Anderson, for the purpose of attesting an affidavit. When they reached the place, said McGarity, they found there Lewis Anderson and William Lawson, a Negro detective, who then requested Anderson to repeat what he had said Boyd Conyers had told him about the Brownsville raid. Anderson, who was an old man, vehemently denied having told Lawson anything about Conyers, said Conyers' name had been mentioned between them but one time, and that was on one occasion when Conyers passed by and Lawson asked him if that was Conyers, and he told him "yes." Anderson further stated that he had had no talk with Conyers, that he had only spoken to him one time, and then only to say "howdy." Lawson insisted on Anderson making an affidavit that Conyers had admitted to him that he knew a great deal more about the shooting at Brownsville than he had told. Lawson insisted that Anderson had told him these things while out fishing. Anderson strongly denied having told Lawson any such thing, and got his Bible and placed his hands on it and denied that he had ever made any such statement to Lawson, or that he had ever had any conversation with Conyers about the matter in any way, calling upon God to strike him dead if he was telling a lie. Anderson refused to make the desired affidavit. Baldwin and Arnold then went to the home of Boyd Conyers. Baldwin asked Conyers if he knew Lawson. Conyers stated that he knew him when he saw him. Baldwin told him that Lawson said he went and made a confession to him on the train in the presence of Lonzo Hennon, and that he, Baldwin, had Hennon's affidavit in his pocket showing this to be true. Conyers replied that he could not help what Baldwin had, that it was not true, that he made no confession to Lawson or to anyone else.

Arnold stated that he was present during all the conversation and heard it all. Conyers positively denied knowing anything about the shooting, stating that he was asleep at the time the shooting took place.

Foraker omitted five additional affidavits, to the same effect, in his Senate speech.

There are some additional bizarre aspects to the Browne episode. For example, despite Foraker's serious challenge, Browne's report was heard again without comment in subsequent months by the Court of Inquiry. According to Foraker, the Court so arranged the order in which Browne was called as to enable him to depart expeditiously "and before any steps could be taken to arrest him."[3] An effort by counsels N. B. Marshall and General Daggett to have Browne resubpoenaed as, said Daggett, "we have information to the effect that he may leave for Cuba at any time," or to have brought before the court correspondence with Foraker offering evidence which contradicted Browne's testimony, was denied.[4]

Efforts to have Browne indicted for perjury seem never to have materialized. A lengthy statement submitted by the associate counsel before the Brownsville Court of Inquiry requested a perjury indictment, offering substantial evidence for its validity. Why it was never acted upon can only be surmised. Perhaps it had something to do with the explanation offered by General Daggett, chief defense counsel before the Brownsville Court of Inquiry. Discussing the impending court-martial of Captain Lyon, he wrote to Foraker that "they have not, in my opinion, a thing against Lyon. But they want to find something to trade on to save Browne. I have seen all along they are much concerned about the Browne matter. I think they fear his prosecution would implicate some of them."[5]

How Herbert Browne originally got to the War Department is itself strange. Browne was originally employed by Foraker. Browne claimed that he was fired because he submitted an unfavorable report. Foraker claimed that Browne was fired because his report was inadequate, that when Browne reported verbally to Foraker in Washington, Foraker realized that he had no information except what he might have gathered from general statements made by the Brownsville citizens, which were of such a character as to show that they were untrustworthy and mere speculation based on what he had been told by Brownsville citizens, and what he might have gathered from reading the testimony that had been taken before the Senate Committee on Military Affairs, all of which was then common knowledge.

Foraker then submitted to the Board of Inquiry a memorandum he stated was written April 9, 1907, to the effect that a J. C. Williams called on the telephone and told him that an H. J. Browne had just given him some very important information with respect to the Brownsville matter and asked if he would like to meet Mr. Browne. He said "yes," and both arrived that evening. Browne then told him that he had learned from a reliable source that the shooting up of Brownsville had been done by seven men who were citizens of that city. Three of them were in Mexico, but four were in or near Brownsville and that for some reason he was not at liberty to explain, these four would be willing to turn State's evidence provided the Governor of Texas would provide executive clemency. He said he did not care to get involved in any way but would, in the interest of justice, undertake to make all arrangements if his expenses were paid and if he were given some reasonable compensation for his time. A few days later Foraker advanced him $500.

Foraker also submitted several letters from Browne written during this period. One, dated April 25, 1907, stated that Louis Cowen, whose house was shot up, was the head devil in this business. "He is a renegade Jew. Russian I am informed, whose real name is Cowajiian, or something like it." He had been conspicuous in his offensive attitude and language toward the Negro troopers. On the question of the rifles, Browne said that the 95 model Winchesters were easily altered to take either the Springfield or Krag cartridge. Besides, members of the disbanded Brownsville troop had Krags, not all of which were turned in. While plenty of empty shells – all Springfields – had been turned in, only three bullets were in evidence, and one of them could have come from a Krag. A slight sharpening of the point of the firing pin would make the Winchester fire the Government ammunition, or again, the spring could be changed, blocked up, or drawn to increase its blow, in a few minutes.

He concluded: "Brownsville doesn't want to frighten off Northern capital and would like to have the whole affair forgotten."

A few days later he wrote:

> I am going out hunting ocelots with Louis Cowen and his gang. I think every one of the prospective party was mixed up in the affray. . . . The way the colored soldiers were harried, annoyed, persecuted and insulted in this town was damnable. The principal offenders, too, were U. S. government officials. It's all another story. . . . The crude way in which the Government handled this whole business is farcical. After the preliminary examination it was all worked to cover and protect Roosevelt.

He wrote that letter on April 27. On May 10 he wrote: "The negro troops shot up the town. I can name four of them. The town gang headed by Cowen had made plans to do them up, but the soldiers got started too quickly." There was, he went on, a tacit understanding between the leading men of Brownsville and the officers to minimize and cover up certain phases of the affair. First, the troops were very much out of control. They were unkempt, disorderly, slouchy and failed to salute their officers. Second, they had a certain number of extra rifles not accounted for. There was gross carelessness in accounting for ammunition. Most of the noncommissioned officers slept apart from the men, and the ones who had the rack keys either hung them up where they were easily accessible or carried them in their pockets where any soldier could get them at night. Third, with two exceptions, every man of the fifteen who shot up the town was a D Company man. Fourth, the townspeople had warning from three sources that the town was to be shot up but paid no heed and failed to warn Major Penrose of the reports. Fifth, the soldiers were subjected to unnecessary annoyances and insults. The local authorities wanted to cover up 4 and 5: the officers wanted to cover up 1 and 2.

With the exception of possibly three desperadoes among the soldiers, there was no intention to do more than give the town a good scare. Nearly all fired in the air. "Three of them had murder in their hearts." Had it not been for the shooting of Natus there would have been plenty of soldiers to come out with the information, but that scared them off.

> But I can show how to get it all out of Lipscomb, Wheeler and Johnson. B and C companies had no part in the raid on the town. The Administration could have got the whole story first hand if it had used anything like ordinary astuteness, and it can get it now. My story came from a negro railroad porter named Dean. . . . There was a meeting of Brownsville toughs before the shooting. Cowen was present. . . . There was another after the shooting, and dynamite was brought in to blow up the barracks, but the town officials headed it off, in view of Penrose's threat to destroy the town if the post was attacked. But I'll wait till I see you. The main thing is, that you can now secure evidence of the guilty, and exonerate the innocent, which is the essential thing.[6]

For whatever reason, Foraker and Browne did not come to terms when they met again. Perhaps it was as Browne claimed, that he came back with the wrong report; perhaps Foraker was justified in claiming that the report was shoddy.

By the following March, Browne had made contact with the Roosevelt Administration and offered his services. A communication to Roosevelt from the Department of the Interior stated that a feeler was received that three persons in Brownsville could identify three of the Negro soldiers who did the shooting. Unfortunately for their general credibility, two of these persons were prostitutes and the other a barkeeper. It appears from the statement made [to me], wrote F. E. Lenpp, author of the communication, that of the fifteen or sixteen soldiers, all except three shot into the air. The three, his informant said, could be positively identified as having deliberately sought to take human life or as being so utterly reckless of it as to be practically guilty of murderous intent. "The man who gives me this information is Herbert J. Browne," a former newspaper correspondent who was engaged to go to Brownsville for the purpose of proving no Negro soldiers did what they were accused of. Browne disappointed his employer by bringing back "the discomforting news" that these particular men had been engaged in just what they were accused of.

". . . if you care to see Mr. Browne I could hunt him up and send him to the White House." The letter had written across it "answered," but there was no copy found in the files. In May of 1908 the War Department entered into negotiations with Browne and on September 1 an agreement was reached that Browne was to report to the War Department the names of the guilty soldiers not later than October 10.

Browne had a vague history; a newspaperman by profession, he was at one time editor of the *Roanoke Times*. He later went to Cuba and laid claim to an uninhabited island off the West Indies, alleged to be rich in natural resources. The sign on the door of his office was "Calapatch Island," and it is supposed that the office was the headquarters of the company he organized to exploit the island. An adventurer and a commercial soldier of fortune, he was indeed an unsavory character for either Foraker or Roosevelt to deal with.[7]

NOTES

1. Found in the Foraker papers.
2. Browne's report, which was examined in typed form in the National Archives, War Department File, 1763692, was published in Albert Bigelow Paine, *Captain Bill McDonald, Texas Ranger: A Story of Frontier Reform* (New York: J.J. Little & Ives Co., 1909), Appendix D, pp. 418-25.
3. Foraker to Bulkeley, May 24, 1910, Foraker papers.
4. Typescript of Record of Brownsville Court of Inquiry, January 11, 1910, furnished by N.B. Marshall, typed form, Foraker papers.
5. April 1, 1910, Foraker papers.
6. Typed letter, Adjutant General's Office, War Department File, 1909.
7. Background material from Associated Counsel's report for Brownsville Inquiry Re quest for Perjury Indictment Against Browne, Foraker paper, 1024.

PART II
THE BLACK COMMUNITY

V

THE BLACK COMMUNITY RESPONDS

Like a cur he's mustered out;
He's thrown out, he's kicked out!
Like a cur he's mustered out
  In Peace's sunny season.
After he has served the land —
Served it long and served it grand,
They kick him out! And, understand,
  Without any reason.

He's good enough when bullets fly,
When bullets fly, when bullets fly!
He's good enough when bullets fly
  To bear the brunt of battle.
He's good enough when bullets fly,
And men are needed for to die,
A country for to glorify!
  Aye, cheer him on to battle.

Like a dog they're mustered out,
Thrown out, kicked out!
Like a dog they've kicked him out

And daubed him with disgrace.
Yet, when Peace hath flown away,
And grim War holdeth bloody sway —
They'll call him in that darksom day
The bullets for to face.[1]

The black community throughout the nation responded to the Brownsville dismissals with extraordinary outrage and anger. The enormous outpouring of protest was astonishing. After all, violence, terror, organized and
otherwise, intimidation — these were the ordinary occurrences for the black
in America. That the Negro community reacted so strongly and so persistently to the Brownsville issue suggests that there was more to it than simple
injustice of a kind the Afro-American had come to know intimately.

This was a case with strong legal grounds. Then too it was the kind of
issue around which it was easy to develop a protest movement. But the black
community seems to have been most enraged because of the humiliations
inflicted upon the Negro as a soldier and a representative of the United States
Government, a position which had hitherto carried with it dignity and respect. Even in uniform, even in the role of protector, the black was to be
selected for discriminatory treatment.

Worse, the attack came not from irresponsible racists, but from a man
viewed formerly as a friend. That Theodore Roosevelt was the vehicle for this
insult made the shock even greater. To be lynched, beaten, refused the vote,
these were acts perpetrated by dreadful men in society. When the friend in
the White House turned against them too, where were the blacks to go for
help? Thus when Senator Foraker defended the Brownsville soldiers he was
uncritically supported. The over anxiety of the Afro-Americans to find allies
and the desperation with which they clung to them is demonstrated by their
blind defense of Foraker.

The black community was genuinely infuriated and shocked. It protested and petitioned and complained and threatened. But where was it to go
and what was it to do? Not vote Republican? Was the Democratic alternative
preferable? The Negro was then, as most Americans were and are, loyal to his
government and could conceive of protest or revolt only within its frame-
work. Although there are now alternatives offered in the black community
outside of the two-party structure, such options were virtually nonexistent in
the early years of the twentieth century.

Booker T. Washington's role in the Brownsville episode was a significant
one. His political strength, while it was substantial within the black community, came from his white allies. His connections to the Republican party
were solid; he was their Negro spokesman and through him was dispensed
whatever patronage was allocated to blacks. Washington opposed Roosevelt's
Brownsville policy and did what he could to dissuade the President from

continuing it. But when Washington's advice was repudiated, his protest ended. Roosevelt had made a mistake, but the issue was closed. At that point Washington began to exert his influence to curtail the protest movement, particularly with the idea of stopping any efforts to desert the Republican ranks.

Washington exerted much pressure on Negro newspapers and leaders, especially religious leaders, but there was not much he could do with popular reaction. It was against him. Brownsville was, in fact, one of the important issues on which the anti-Washington movement was forged. It provided both the excuse for those already in opposition to attack him vigorously and the issue on which many supporters deserted him. With his shrewd insight, Washington knew that the best way to handle Brownsville was to ignore it and watch the controversy slowly crumble, which it ultimately did.

How does one gauge a community response? Newspaper reactions, letters-to-the-editor, public meetings, statements of race leaders, assessment by the opposition? By all such measures, the Brownsville episode rocked the black community.

The issue took such clear-cut form because of its intimate and organic association with the political life of the nation. The villains were Roosevelt and then Taft, and the hero was Foraker, who made a bid for the presidency. Here was a rare opportunity for the anger of the blacks to take political form and for their threats of desertion from Republican ranks to be tested at the polls. Although in retrospect it is clear that there was no real danger to the Republican machine, there was, at the time, good reason for the Republicans and Booker T. Washington to worry.

In earlier years, especially after the Booker T. Washington dinner, blacks attended, in large numbers, the President's annual reception. But in January, 1907, The Birmingham *Herald* reported, the "blacks all but boycotted" the reception. Of the thousands in line, "very few were negroes." The general attendance was "also less than ordinary", "as many white people remained away from the reception owing to the usually large negro gathering." The small black attendance "is attributed to the Brownsville incident."[2]

In the House and Senate, on the other hand, black attendance was increasing markedly. "No man in recent years has received the ovation that was given Senator Foraker," reported the *Washington Post*, "when he concluded his speech in defense of the Brownsville soldiers."

Never, within the history of the Senate, have there been so many colored persons within the Senate galleries.[3]

Such scenes had been going on for months, for earlier that year a similar report from the New York *Age* claimed that "One must go back for a generation" to parallel such scenes as had occurred during the previous weeks at the

Capitol.

> The galleries of the Senate are crowded with eager throngs of people of
> both races. . . . It has been the one great subject which has engrossed
> the colored people of Washington during this time. . . .there has plainly
> occurred a recrudescence of the race question in the country.

Expressing great optimism, the newspaper concluded:

> Almost it appears to us at times as if the colored people were at the end
> of the long and miserable lane of this reactionary period in the Republic,
> so close at moments seem the movement, the path which is to carry
> them back to their lost rights under the Constitution through the power-
> ful aid of a regenerated public opinion in the North.[4]

The Negro "has never been so rebellious as at the present time," wrote a
Pennsylvania newspaper.[5]

A long report, typical of many such others, was sent to Booker T.
Washington from a loyal Chicago supporter shortly after the Brownsville
incident occurred. "Things in Chicago are at fever heat on the race matter,"
he wrote. "You cannot find a Negro who is not denouncing the President in
frightful terms of abuse. I never saw and heard anything like it." Mass meetings are held, he went on, in which the President's acts and motives are
attacked. The newspapers are giving much space to the matter, and are com-
menting "on the extraordinary coming together of the Negro people for
defensive and offensive purposes." He further reported a "highly sensational"
sermon preached the previous Sunday by Dr. A. J. Casey to an overflowing
audience. Both he and his audience forgot that it was Sunday and the place
was a church. "Every point of attack against the President was cheered to the
echo. The whole performance was an unworthy one, both for the day and the
place." The letter-writer's own opinion was that while he was pained to see
the battalion dismissed, he did not view the matter as an attack on the race.
He concluded with a hope that the President will be able to convince the
people of this fact, for if he fails to do so and the present feeling continues,
"he will become the worst hated man who has been president in 50 years."[6]

Another confidante, R. W. Thompson, wrote from Kentucky to Washington's secretary, Emmett J. Scott, that "Roosevelt is 'in bad' here on account of the firing of those Negro soldiers."[7] Thompson wrote again the
following week saying:

> Sorry Roosevelt has made the mistake of his life. We are giving him a
> chance to put the blame on Garlington . . . . In but few instances since
> the South scared him to death over the Washington dinner and the
> Indianola incident, has he manifested the cocksureness of other years on
> the race question.

And again, if he does not rescind the order, "his name will be anathema with
the Negroes from now on."

Thompson publicly aired his views in his column in the widely read Indianapolis *Freeman*. "Press and public among the Afro-Americans of the country are stirred to their depths, expressions both radical and conservative are heard in shops, homes and on the curbstones, and the tenor is unanimous that the punishment . . . is unnecessarily severe."[8]

Thompson was probably correct when he said that Brownsville was an issue on which there was no moderate-radical division. The division was between those committed to the Republican Party and everyone else. At the 1907 convention of the moderate Afro-American Council, Bishop Walters, its president, expressed approval for Roosevelt's stand in behalf of fair play, but "regrets" his discharge of 167 soldiers without "any competent legal evidence of guilt," and prays that he will exercise his "characteristic courage in correcting this great wrong."[9] The convention was called, the Council declared, to examine "the timid and uncertain stand of those who essay to befriend us, even to President Roosevelt who has said so much about 'fair play' and the 'door of hope,' but who has delt us a severe blow in the dismissal of the colored soldiers."[10]

Throughout 1907 and 1908 the black newspapers were filled with reports of meetings and petitions protesting the dismissal of the troops. At the general conference of the A.M.E. Church in New York in November, 1906, Roosevelt was vigorously attacked by several of the ministers. The President is no longer a friend, many said, for he has altered his attitude toward the black: witness his response to the Afro-American soldiers who "clashed recently with white brutes of Brownsville."[11] Dr. J. R. White attacked Roosevelt for overlooking the misdeeds of white troops who during the riot in Atlanta assaulted Negroes and invaded their homes.[12]

Rev. W. Bishop Johnson, pastor of the Second Baptist Church, colored, Washington, D.C., condemned the President. The church was crowded, and at the conclusion of his address there were prolonged cheers. A party of Howard University students gave a college yell. Roosevelt's order, said the minister, puts a premium on the traitor. The guilty should be punished, he said, making the assumption that the soldiers were guilty, but the innocent should not have been made to suffer. He ended by blaming the War Department for having put these men "in the enemy's territory."[13] The responsibility for discovering the guilty men should have been the Secret Service's, not the soldiers'.[14]

The newspapers reported that the Union Republican Club of Cincinnati denounced Roosevelt;[15] meetings of the Ministerial Association of Colored Preachers, the Baptist Ministers, and the Clergical Union of Long Island opposed the President's action;[16] the Charles Sumner Afro-American League of Picqua, Ohio, was formed on the Brownsville issue;[17] Thomas L. Jones, an attorney, criticized the dismissal at a meeting of the National Anti-Jim Crow

Bar Association;[18] the Colored Baptist Ministerial Conference of Philadelphia passed a resolution expressing grateful appreciation to Senator Foraker for his work in behalf of the colored soldiers;[19] the New Jersey chapter of the Constitution League was formed to deal with the Brownsville issue;[20] two protest meetings were held in Chicago in one week to attack Taft, the Republican candidate, the Republican Party in general and Booker T. Washington;[21] the Afro-American Suffrage League of Boston passed several resolutions denouncing Roosevelt on the Brownsville affair and describing his actions as worthy of Nero or the Duke of Alva.[22]

In Washington on one November Sunday two sermons were delivered in black churches denouncing Roosevelt: The Cosmopolitan Baptist Church and the Second Baptist Church.[23] The New England Suffrage League protested to Roosevelt his handling of the case.[24] In the early months of 1907, seventy-two citizens of Trenton, New Jersey, appealed to Congress to authorize a thorough investigation; sixty-three residents of Bordentown, New Jersey, did the same. Petitions also came in from Camden, New Jersey; Pueblo, Colorado; Cape May City, New Jersey. Mass meetings were held at Cooper Union in New York; the Republican Club of De Moines, Iowa; and Providence, Rhode Island.[25] At the December, 1906, meeting of the Colored Ministers Interdenomination Alliance, after heated debate, resolutions were adopted denouncing Roosevelt. Dr. J. G. Robinson, pastor of Young's Chapel, A.M.E. Church "created something of a sensation" by remarking that for the first time in twenty-five years he held no Thanksgiving service in his church. "I did not want to desecrate the house of God by holding a service proclaimed by a man like Theodore Roosevelt."[26] At a Union Thanksgiving service in which members of four black churches participated, Roosevelt was denounced for his role in the Brownsville episode. Nearly everyone present made a contribution to a fund for relief of the soldiers.[27] The Methodist bishops "on the whole notable for their conservatism," but who "could at times be moved to dignified but resolute protest,"[28] issued a statement at a conference of bishops in February 1908. Protesting against the "monstrous injustices" involved in the Brownsville incident and the lily-white policies of the Administration,[29] they warned the Republicans not to nominate either Roosevelt or Taft.[30]

The North Carolina Negro Baptists Association denounced the President. At a meeting in Washington to protest his action, the audience refused to sing "America." Calvin Chase, editor of the *Washington Bee*, who was a Roosevelt delegate to the Philadelphia convention of 1900, made a bitter speech against him.[31] A call was issued by a group of Texans for an organization of colored citizens, patterned after the Ohio Afro-American League formed the previous May.

The Brownsville imbroglio in Texas affords us the opportunity of announcing to the world our convictions and aligning forces for a triumphant campaign against the combined armies of hatred, prejudice and indifference toward us within the party ranks.

Referring to Foraker as the best and truest friend, it said that it is now "up to our people to show their mark of appreciation."[32] Almost 400 people at a meeting at the Antioch Baptist Church in Cleveland signed a petition deploring the hasty act of President Roosevelt and requesting Congress to adopt Senator Foraker's inquiry resolution.[33] More than 100 persons signed a petition from Painesville, Ohio, to show their appreciation to Foraker "for the good he has done for the Brownsville soldiers and also for the colored people in general."[34] The colored citizens of Wheeling, West Virginia, commended Senator N.B. Scott in his "endeavor to procure for the colored soldiers a fair and impartial judgement."[35] The Du Bois Circle of the Niagara Movement of Maryland submitted to Foraker an expression of their deep appreciation for his "magnificent effort to secure justice and fair play for the discharged soldiers of the 25th Infantry when no one else dared to speak in their behalf."[36] The Sumner League, a Republican organization of black voters in Indianapolis, Indiana, wrote to Foraker pledging him support.[37]

A supporter and a friend of Washington's, Ralph Tyler from the *Ohio State Journal* in Columbus, Ohio, spoke out against the "intemperate utterances of Negro ministers and cheap politicians," and complained that in Ohio "the Negroes are depleting the dictionary of adjectives in their denunciation of the President, and throughout the north the Negro ministers and politicians have seized upon the affair to attract attention to them."[38] Even his own loyal support, he went on, is not based upon the case itself, for "on the face of things their dismissal appears unprecedented and without warrant." Rather, in the absence of satisfactory data, he suspended judgment as "I cannot bring myself to believe the President would act against the race. His course has been so fair and just heretofore."

Foraker received extensive mail supporting and encouraging him. The letters came, in large part, from blacks in positions of influence and prominence: pastors of churches, lawyers, doctors, dentists, insurance company heads, funeral directors, editors, businessmen, elementary and high school principals. Most letters were typed and many of those were on stationery from the United States Treasury Department, the Interstate Commerce Commission, the Post Office in Washington, D.C. as well as in local areas and the Department of Interior. Civil servants, at least initially, were apparently willing to criticize the President.

The response of the black community as a whole toward the Administration's handling of the Brownsville episode resulted in two significant repercussions, although the first proved to be only temporary — a disaffection with the Republican party and a disaffection with Booker T. Washington.

The repudiation of Roosevelt and therefore Washington gave encouragement to the burgeoning anti-Washington forces, and indeed, caused many former loyal supporters to break with him. Those who defended Washington and Roosevelt were subjected to grave pressures from their constituency, whether that constituted readers, students, congregations or voters.

The agony of one such loyal supporter, Abraham Grant, presiding bishop and President of the Financial Board of the Fifth Episcopal District, A.M.E. Church, from Kansas, is reflected in the lengthy correspondence he carried on with Washington on the subject of Brownsville. It began shortly after the dismissal order. "I write to say that I am almost out of heart and discouraged this morning. . . . It is so unlike him to do a thing of this kind; it is so unreasonable; it is so detrimental to the interests of the colored people. Even Grover Cleveland would not have issued such an order. What on earth is the matter with him," he asked? "Why don't you go to see him and talk with him and try to keep him a friend to the weak and helpless of the nation?"[39] Later the same month Bishop Grant wrote again to Washington that he did not remember when he had had "anything to knock me off my feet" so completely as the President's order. Bishop Grant assumed the soldiers' guilt (they were "not wholly responsible for the trouble") but, he claimed, there could be no inside facts, as Washington asserted, to warrant discharging those faithful and innocent men who had served their country "because of the conduct of others; and even the men who used their guns simply retaliated."[40]

Washington replied as he did to all such critics: he had made several attempts to dissuade the President from his action. Roosevelt is too big a man, Washington went on, to let conditions remain, and he will no doubt soon reinstate himself into "the love and good wishes of our race."[41]

The following year Bishop Grant wrote to Foraker and suggested a particular witness be called before the Senate committee. "It is gratifying to know," he ended one letter "that you are determined that the country shall know the truth in the matter, and none should be satisfied with less."[42]

Nevertheless, Bishop Grant's relations with Washington remained warm and loyal. Scanning the correspondence between the two, it is clear that Bishop Grant was not only in the Washington camp, but in it actively, to the point of reporting to Washington on meetings he attended. Yet on the Brownsville issue he would not fall in line.

> With reference to my being against President Roosevelt and Mr. Taft, I beg to say that I have never permitted myself to say a word against President Roosevelt, except with reference to the Brownsville affair, and

that was not to be published. I have made it clear that I believed that his heart was right, but that he was misled by others in that case.[43]

If Bishop Grant remained loyal to Washington, in spite of Brownsville, Archibald Grimké seems to have made his decision to break with him on the same issue. Grimké presided over the "aristocracy of the intellectuals," the American Negro Academy, and "to some extent" reflected the view of Washington. On the other hand, he was soon associated with the William Trotter group and became president of the anti-Washington Boston Literary and Historical Society.[44] At first he vacillated, moving from one camp to the next, and back. At one point Washington benefited from the difficult personality of W. E. B. Du Bois, who insulted Grimké. As a result, Grimké seemed "more than anxious to line up with us," having "broken off completely from Du Bois and his crowd," according to Washington. As treasurer of the Committee of Twelve, Grimké acted as an intermediary between Washington, who secretly supplied the funds, and ex-Senator Henry W. Blair, in securing the latter's services as a lobbyist against the Warner-Foraker amendment to the Hepburn Railway Act. This amendment, by requiring equality of accommodations in interstate travel, would have by implication condoned segregation throughout the country, under the separate-but-equal doctrine.[45] On Brownsville, however, Grimké joined the opposition. August Meier believes "this may have been the turning point in his relations with Washington."[46]

Washington's loyal supporter, Anderson, reported Grimké as "savagely denouncing" the President, the Secretary of War and Washington at a meeting in 1908. From then on, Grimké was "distinctly of the opposition." He became active in the N.A.A.C.P., where he served as President of the Washington, D.C. branch, rejected Washington's views on suffrage, "and forthrightly attacked all forms of discrimination."[47]

Foraker saved a highly laudatory letter from Grimké, written in April, 1908:

> Though your enemies and the enemies of the Negro race may succeed in retiring you from public official life, as is threatened, they can never wipe out the great record that you have made. . . . The real victor in every struggle is the man who fights on the side of right.[48]

Mary Church Terrell was another supporter of Washington's who grew increasingly critical of his policies in general and ultimately broke with him on the Brownsville question. As late as the fall of 1906 she was working closely with Washington, but later the same year she implicitly challenged him when she criticized Negro leaders who tell "dialect stories, counsel an inferior sort of education and advise accommodation" to southern discrimination.[49] She was reported as saying privately that she intended to "unshirt" Washington.[50] But the final split with Washington was reached when she defended the Brownsville soldiers and supported the Constitution League. Early in 1907 she wrote to Foraker:

> How can I, how can any member of the race with which I am identified, find words adequate to convey to you the gratitude we feel for your eloquent and courageous words in behalf of justice which you uttered in the Senate today. I cannot begin to tell you how your appeal stirred my heart and I have heard a score or more say the same thing.[51]

Even her husband, generally more moderate, was reported "shocked at Washington's actions" toward those who defended the discharged soldiers, and Anderson thought that "Judge Terrell had better take a stitch in his tongue." He believed that Terrell was "Washington's man" when the "Doctor is around, and yet he manages to give his approval and support to all of his enemies."[52]

John Milholland, too, was originally a supporter of Washington's and worked with him informally on many matters. It was the Brownsville situation that led to a permanent break.[53]

The Afro-American Council, which replaced T. T. Fortune's defunct Afro-American League in 1898, and became the leading civil rights organization prior to 1905, maintained the earlier organization's conciliatory and moderate point of view, and passed under the control of Washington after the turn of the century. During 1901 and 1902 Washington anonymously contributed to the legal bureau, and was, in fact, "clandestinely directing its course of action." At the 1902 St. Paul convention "the Washington group secured Fortune's election as president over determined opposition. The convention's manifesto was even more conciliatory than usual, and the elected officials were almost entirely in the Washington orbit." As Emmett J. Scott said, "We control the Council now."[54]

As the repercussions following the Brownsville incident mounted, Washington became increasingly concerned about his power over the Council. At the convention in the fall of 1906, although the Council was split over the Brownsville issue and the Atlanta riot, Washington was able, for the moment at least, to maintain his authority. Soon, however, the Council's position was "directly at variance"[55] with Washington's. While Washington was actively engaged in convincing others to minimize the incident, several of the leaders of the Council offered their support to Foraker in his fight in behalf of the soldiers.[56]

The Niagara Movement, as one would expect, denounced Roosevelt's actions and wholeheartedly endorsed Foraker. Wrote Du Bois to Foraker early in 1907:

> On my own behalf and in the name of the Niagara Movement, I wish to thank you very heartily for the work which you have done in behalf of

the colored soldiers. I trust that you will realize that the colored people of the United States appreciate this service and will always look upon your efforts with the greatest gratitude.[57]

But Du Bois, alone among black leaders then and later, never changed his early opinion that the soldiers were guilty. In *Dusk at Dawn*, published in 1940, he commented:

I saw in Asia and the West Indies the results of race discrimination while right here in America came the wild foray of the exasperated Negro soldiers at Brownsville.

Eight years later he referred to the "needless severity" with which the soldiers were punished "who were accused of having revolted under the greatest provocation at Brownsville, Texas, in 1906."[58]

The Niagara Movement Conference in August, 1907 sent telegrams of support to Foraker and to the Constitution League for "turning the searchlight of truth upon the national administration's act of brutal injustice to our soldiers and for the tireless endeavor to efface that new stain upon our country's honor."[59]

The issue continued to be of importance, for at the 1908 Conference in Oberlin the

Negroes of the Niagara Movement. . .presented a brief address to the negroes of the country. . . .

"We say to voters: Register and vote whenever and wherever you have a right. . . .Remember that the conduct of the Republican party toward negroes has been a disgraceful failure to keep just promises. The dominant Roosevelt faction has sinned in this respect beyond forgiveness. We therefore trust that every black voter will uphold men like Joseph Benson Foraker, and will leave no stone unturned to defeat William H. Taft. Remember Brownsville, and establish next November the principle of negro independence in voting, not only for punishing enemies but for rebuking false friends."[60]

The Afro-American was a loyal American and a loyal Republican. He had withstood many provocations without threatening to desert the Republican party. Part of the problem, of course, was that he had no place else to go. The Democratic party was intimately associated with the white South; it was not until the emergence of Franklin D. Roosevelt that any significant desertion from Republican ranks took place. Third parties have traditionally found little appeal among Americans and even less within the black community. But in 1906, as a result of the Brownsville situation, there appeared to be a genuine threat of disaffection: first, not to support Taft for the nomination, and then not to support the party at the general election when Taft was nominated. It was the involvement of Joseph B.

Foraker, a national political figure, that turned the threat of disaffection into a political possibility.

Roosevelt immediately recognized the political implications. After reading and approving the recommendation to discharge all the soldiers, he did not release the order to the public until November 7, 1906, the day after the election in which Republicans retained control of the House of Representatives. The Waterville (Maine) *Sentinel* declared that in many northern districts black voters had held the balance for the Republicans because of their personal devotion to Roosevelt.

> They did not care so much for the local candidates. It was a case of "we are coming brother Theodore, three hundred thousand strong," but they would have been coming in different temper had they known that on brother Theodore's desk was an order to disgrace and humiliate the entire colored battalion of the 25th Infantry.

The *Sentinel* charged that the President's action did "more credit to his adroitness than to his frankness" and the picture of a president whose chief merit is supposed to lie in his fearless bravery dodging an issue like this one, until after the votes are counted, is not pleasant to look upon, even though it stamps him as a clever politician.[61]

Typical was the attack from Rev. W. Bishop Johnson, pastor of the Second Baptist Church, colored, in November 1906, when he said:

> Had the order dismissing the Twenty-fifth been issued a few days earlier, the result of the election in New York would have been vastly different. Unless things alter considerably, there is going to be a big change, politically, in this country, and a new party, greater than any yet known, will rise up.[62]

At the Abyssinian Baptist Church the minister also made a political threat.

> The President's decree was signed the day after the election. He shot us when our gun was empty. But we have two years to work, and our slogan shall be "A Republican Congress to protect our people in the South, a Democratic President to resent the insult heaped upon us." Thus shall we answer Theodore Roosevelt, once enshrined in our hearts as Moses, now enshrined in our scorn as Judas.[63]

Bishop Grant offered his analysis in a letter to Washington.

> The republican and independent press in all this section of the country is in sympathy with the troops, and the President has given the democratic party one of the best campaign documents that they have had since the Civil War and it may be that his party will lose the next national election, for certainly the colored people in the doubtful states will

remember this. He will also have a fight on his hands in Congress. For I have a communication before me from one of the strongest men in the senate who states that he is as much surprised and disappointed as I am and intimates his course when the opportunity comes.[64]

The *Age* reported a meeting of 200 of the Regular Colored Republican organization of the 9th Assembly district, New York, in which "President Roosevelt's name, which has heretofore always been good for a round of applause in any gathering of Afro-Americans . . . this time . . . was received with a dead silence." The group then passed resolutions denouncing Roosevelt and stating that he would never receive their votes again.[65] A meeting in Louisville, Kentucky, endorsed the position of the Washington, D.C. Negroes not to support Taft. Resolutions were passed denouncing the dismissal of the soldiers, opposing the nomination of Taft or any man who rejects Negro enfranchisement.[66] When the Republicans of Kentucky, in their convention, adopted a resolution favoring the nomination for President of a candidate in full accord with the President, but not naming Secretary Taft specifically, some analysts inferred their unwillingness to cite him was due to the opposition of blacks because of the Brownsville case.[67]

The *Washington Post* reported a meeting at which two thousand Negro delegates from across the nation hissed the names of Taft and Roosevelt, supported Foraker for President and named Hughes as an acceptable candidate. Bishop Walters presided.[68] A large meeting at the Bethel A.M.E. Church passed resolutions attacking Taft and supporting Foraker's Brownsville position.[69] A group of Washington, D.C. Negroes heard a letter read from Bishop Walters attacking Taft and Roosevelt. It ended with the words, ". . . I believe we should [do] . . . everything in our power to defeat the perpetrators of the outrage."[70] The Afro-American League of Shawnee County, Kansas, met in group to denounce Roosevelt, oppose the Taft nomination, support Foraker, and urge the colored people all over Kansas to act politically to enforce their decisions.[71]

The Negro Republican League of Kansas formed a permanent state organization on April 7, 1908, on the following platform:

1) Uphold the Declaration of Independence;

2) Uphold the principles upon which the Republican Party was founded;

3) Recognize the danger the present administration has placed the Negro in by encouraging the South to pass state Jim Crow laws;

4) Condemn Roosevelt on Brownsville as the greatest wrong to our race that has ever been done by any President of this nation;

5) Support P.P. Campbell of the 3rd congressional district for his courage in regard to the colored race;

6) Support Foraker as the nominee at Chicago.[72]

A North Carolina Negro Republican state convention was held in May, 1908, "as a protest against the treatment of negroes by the white Republicans." Eight congressional districts were represented by fifty Negro delegates. Foraker was endorsed for the presidency and his course in defense of the Brownsville soldiers was commended.[73]

The *Cleveland Gazette* devoted much editorial space to the question of disaffection. It quoted at length a statement by the editors of the *Philadelphia Daily Record* to the effect that claims that blacks will repudiate Taft are made by friends of rival Republican candidates in the faint hope of thus preventing his nomination. "But let him be nominated and the colored brethren would be second only to the trusts in the enthusiasm of their support of the ticket," the Philadelphia newspaper stated. Don't you believe any such "silly thing," commented the *Gazette* – at least as far as the blacks in Ohio are concerned. What is true in Ohio is no doubt true throughout the country, particularly in the North. Eugene V. Debs, the Socialist candidate for president, will get all those votes not cast for Bryan, should Taft or Roosevelt be nominated, the newspaper continued. "And we say this, too, as a lifelong Republican, active for nearly 25 years." Thousands of Afro-Americans will not vote at all, the Ohio editorial went on, and the Republican nominee, if it is Roosevelt or Taft, will go down to certain defeat "as did the Republican candidate for mayor of Cleveland, Congressman Theodore F Burton, last fall, and for the same reasons."[74]

While those who opposed Taft and Roosevelt did so largely on the Brownsville issue, the charges against Taft went back many years. Grimké, in an address in the spring of 1907, presented the case, used many times over, against Taft.

William H. Taft, he began, while ambitious and adroit and able, is a "pliant tool of President Roosevelt. . . .and a pliant tool likewise of American color-prejudice." While he was governor-general of the Philippines "the lie was invented. . .that the Filipinos did not want to have colored troops among them." Taft heeded this lie, this "outrageous outburst of American colorphobia 8,000 miles away from its home" and so secured an order for the recall of all the colored soldiers in the Philippine Islands.

Then, later, when Roosevelt issued his "Draconian order" discharging the Brownsville soldiers, the Secretary of War "with the instinct of a just judge" suspended the order for twenty-four hours.

But when our big War Secretary who is in every inch of his body a. politician, had slept on what he had done and dreamt of the ill consequences which were likely to flow therefrom to his aspirations for the Presidency to succeed his autocratic chief, he repented speedily in the morning and revoked with surprising alacrity his order of suspension.

When Roosevelt called upon him to defend the order of discharge, Taft, "with a mental and moral suppleness which was most amazing," outdid even the author of the unjust order. Even more, he reversed his earlier position that he had held as governor-general in the Philippines, and as a punishment, exiled to the Philippines every colored soldier in the regular army of the United States.

"Pliancy thy name is indeed William H. Taft."

When Roosevelt wanted some man to go South and say a smooth word, make an indirect and adroit defense of southern disfranchisement of the Negro and the "lily-white" movement in those states, whom did he choose to go on this delicate mission, Grimké asked? "Who but his big and pliant Secretary of War."

And finally, when Roosevelt wanted a man to go South and give industrial education for colored people a boom and at the same time damn with faint praise, with American pity, the higher education of the colored people, whom did he select to do this work? "Why no other than his big and pliant Secretary of War, who went to Tuskegee and did exactly what his masterful and autocratic chief expected him to do. And now he is to be rewarded for all his pliancy to that chief and American race prejudice at our ruinous cost by the greatest position in the Republic."

Grimké ended by asking: "Will the colored people help to reward such a pliant tool in the hands of their enemies as has been Mr. Secretary Taft? No, Never! you say, and you say well."[75]

Bishop Derrick called a mass meeting at Cooper Union in New York City for support of Taft, but there was not a great outpouring of black supporters nor any great demonstration for the Secretary of War. While the speakers were all for Taft, the *Washington Post* reported, the crowd gave unmistakable evidence in their applause that they were all for Foraker. Bishop Derrick said he had called the meeting not with the idea of favoring any particular candidate, but to get an answer to the question: Can the American Negro take refuge in the Democratic party? After announcing the question, Bishop Derrick and the other speakers proceeded to eulogize Taft. Their answer to the Foraker cheers was to urge their brethren to "stand by the Grand Old Party even if it's Taft."[76]

In the spring of 1908 the anti-Taft movement took organizational form with the establishment of the National Negro-American Political League of the United States which met and endorsed Foraker for President and attacked Taft and Roosevelt on Brownsville. The organization issued a call April, 1908 for a national political suffrage conference of colored Americans. It was signed by Alexander Walters, President of the Afro-American Council; William H. Scott, President of the Suffrage League of Boston and vicinity; and William Monroe Trotter, President of the New England Constitution and Suffrage League. The call was issued, said a leaflet, because of the approach of the party nominating conventions and the "notoriously hostile attitude" of the present Republican Administration toward its citizens of color. The statement referred to the open alliance between the President and the white southern Democrats who are nullifying the Constitution; to the branding of Negroes by the President as concealors of criminals and rapists,[77] while defaming and discharging in disgrace more than 100 soldiers, all colored, without a trial or chance to be heard in their own defense. The conference, called for April 7, 1908, in Philadelphia "will establish demands to be made of political parties."[78]

This group, reported to consist of representatives from organizations including the Afro-American Council, the Niagara Movement, and the Constitution League, "took a strong stand against Roosevelt. At its stormy convention," Trotter, Walters and the radical clergymen S. L. Corothers and J. Milton Waldron of Washington, "emerged as the nucleus of the organization."[79] In a statement of purpose, the League claimed to be a confederation of twenty national, state and district political organizations of "intelligent, independent and race-loving Colored men" who wished to organize to use their ballots to secure for the race every right guaranteed it under the Constitution. While it described itself as a political organization, it was neither Republican nor Democratic; it was independent in politics and sought to have its members vote for the measures, the men and the party which would best conserve the interests of the race.

But, the League asserted, the Republican party — the party with which most Negroes have affiliated in the past — had deserted the principles of Lincoln, Grant and Sumner and become tools of corporations, designing politicians and predatory wealth; and its representatives in Congress had refused to pass the Foraker bill for the restoration of the discharged innocent soldiers; and the Chicago Republican convention had placed its approval upon lily-whitism in the South; and the Republican party had approved southern disfranchisement constitutional amendments; and it had, under the leadership of President Roosevelt, determined to eliminate the Negro from politics. The League advised its members, and all other black voters, to vote for William Jennings Bryan, as the most effective way of rebuking the Republican party and securing justice and proper recognition.

Every vote cast by a black man for William J. Bryan, the leaflet continued, would be one vote cast for the manhood and political rights of the race and two votes cast against William H. Taft and the Roosevelt policies. Every vote cast by a black man for the Socialist, the Independence or Prohibition parties would be one vote cast for the manhood and political rights of the race and a half vote cast against Taft.[80] Some forty persons appeared as officers, including David Murray, Du Bois and Grimké. The first convention was a rather sorry affair, attended by fewer than fifty persons. All those present pledged themselves to support Bryan if Taft were nominated. Despite their small numbers, however, the leaders of the organization agitated and influenced beyond their size.[81] For example, the League sponsored many meetings. One in Washington had an audience of more than five hundred.[82]

In a detailed study of the Brownsville episode and the black vote, Emma Lou Thornbrough described how, as it became evident that Taft, and not Foraker, would receive the nomination in 1908, opposition within the leadership of the black community collapsed. Although there were more blacks attending the Republican nominating convention at Chicago in June 1908 than in years passed, and although radicals such as Waldron asserted that if Roosevelt or Taft were nominated the black contingent would withdraw and run an independent candidate, it was Thornbrough's opinion that the anti-Taft movement had already fallen apart.[83]

The radicals did not go down without a fight, however. For example, Waldron was described by the press as "one of the colored preachers who have been here for a week past addressing meetings in the colored churches. Bishop Parks and Bishop Walters, both colored, have been among these speakers, and they have been talking to crowds of colored folks nightly." Aside from the Brownsville matter, what these men seem to hold particularly against Taft is his attitude toward the disfranchisement of the Negro in the South. They say, the Washington paper continued, that unless they can bring about an independent party to be headed by some such man as Senator Foraker, they will keep up the fight against Taft that they have been making here, and they will try to get "every colored voter in the Northern states to vote for the Democratic candidates. How seriously this threat should be taken is a matter of doubt."[84]

A black newspaper observed that "the Jews and the Irishmen divide their votes between the various political parties of the country, and in this way have secured justice and proper recognition at the hands of these parties. Why should not the negro do the same thing?"[85]

A few outstanding leaders did support Bryan publicly. Du Bois, for instance, offered the most sophisticated explanation for his endorsement of the Democrats. Initially he repudiated both major parties to support the Socialist party but then he later decided that Bryan's inactivity was preferable to the position of the "Coward of Brownsville." It was his hope that if the black vote, which held a balance of power in twelve northern states, was utilized properly it might end "the impossible alliance of radical and socialistic Democracy at the North with an aristocratic caste party at the South."[86]

After the election, the National Negro-American Political League, renamed the National Independent Political League, remained active under the leadership of Walters and Niagaraites like Waldron, Trotter and Byron

Gunner, though it apparently had little influence.

In her study, Thornbrough tested the political response of the black community as it expressed itself in elections held in northern cities. In Ohio, where the interest was concentrated, Taft and Foraker fought over control of the delegation to be sent to the nominating convention. Results of an election in Columbus were not encouraging to Foraker, for the Foraker candidate for mayor "was reported to have received fewer than 300 out of a possible 4,000" black votes. In Cleveland, on the other hand, the Taft forces were unsettled. The candidate for mayor, Representative Theodore E. Burton ran with the support of Roosevelt and Taft and was defeated. "Of the two wards in which blacks were most numerous, one went Republican, as it had in the past, but the other gave Johnson a majority."[87]

In Boston a Republican mayor was elected, "despite strenuous efforts to capitalize on the Brownsville issue." Booker T. Washington, who had worked for the Republican candidate, assured the President "that he no longer thought the Brownsville affair would hurt Taft's presidential candidacy."[88]

Republican advisors were not altogether convinced. "In Northern cities," Thornbrough pointed out, "Republican party strategists instructed their speakers to answer hecklers who attempted to raise the Brownsville issue by simply calling attention to the Democratic record instead of trying to justify the discharge of the colored troops."[89] The "Democratic record," as Thornbrough outlined it, might indeed have discouraged disaffections by blacks in large numbers to the Democratic cause. Many Democrats publicly endorsed Roosevelt's discharge of the troops; William Jennings Bryan defended the disfranchisement of southern blacks;[90] the Democratic state convention of West Virginia included in its platform a call for separate accomodations in transportation and a demand for a constitutional amendment rescinding the ballot to "a race inferior in intelligence;" both houses of the Tennessee legislature commended Roosevelt for his action in Brownsville.[91]

Taft won easily, although neither his popular vote nor his electoral vote was as large as Roosevelt's had been in 1904. . . .That Taft's margin of victory in certain northern states – Pennsylvania, Ohio, Indiana and Illinois – was smaller than Roosevelt's may have been due in part to the loss of Negro votes. But the outcome did not reflect a personal antipathy to Taft since he ran ahead of other Republican candidates in those states. Ohio, where it was feared that the Negro feeling against him was especially strong, gave him its electoral votes but elected a Democratic governor. Taft also carried the neighboring state of Indiana, where both a Democratic governor and legislature were elected. Moreover, in New York, where efforts to turn Negroes against him had been particularly strenuous, Taft won by a larger margin than had Roosevelt, and he also ran well ahead of the gubernatorial candidate, Hughes. He also carried

New Jersey, which had a sizable Negro vote, by a larger margin than had Roosevelt. From all this it appears that the Brownsville episode did not lead to a marked defection from the Republican party, nor did Taft appear to have suffered personally because of his part in the affair.[92]

That Roosevelt's order did not result in the disaffection that at first loomed was due to the pressure exerted by Booker T. Washington, the conservative nature of the Negro community, the collapse of the black press or any other potential source of leadership, the withdrawal of Foraker at a crucial moment, some conciliatory efforts of the Republicans, and the unwillingness of the Democratic party to capitalize on the discontent. If the Democratic party did not offer a reasonable alternative, how was the disaffection of the black voter to be channeled? Alternatives outside of the two parties were inconceivable for any but a few of the intellectuals like Du Bois, and even he ended by supporting Bryan. The pity was that the Afro-American was truly in a dilemma. In the face of two unpleasant alternatives, there seemed no reason for the black voter not to remain where he was traditionally more comfortable.

NOTES

1. From the *Washington Bee*, December 1, 1906.
2. The *Herald* (Birmingham, Ala.), January 2, 1907, clipping in the Booker T. Washington papers, Library of Congress, Scrapbook, 1907, Box 1046.
3. April 15, 1908, p. 4.
4. January 24, 1907, p. 1 and jump to all of p. 2.
5. *The News* (New Castle, Pa.), June 15, 1908, Washington papers, Scrapbook, 1908.
6. S. L. Williams to B. T. Washington, November 26, 1906, Washington papers.
7. November 12, 1906, Washington papers.
8. The *Freeman* (Indianapolis), July 13, 1907, p. 4.
9. *Ibid.*
10. Announcement of 10th annual meeting of the National Afro-American Council, the *Freeman*, June 1, 1907, p. 3.
11. The *Cleveland Gazette*, November 3, 1906, p. 2. At this time guilt was assumed.
12. *Ibid.*
13. *Washington Post*, November 14, 1906, p. 2.
14. *Washington Bee*, November 17, 1906, p. 5.
15. The *Age*, November 15, 1906, p. 1.
16. *Washington Post*, November 18, 1906, p. 4.
17. The *Freeman*, November 30, 1907, p. 1.
18. *Washington Bee*, December 1, 1906, p. 1.
19. Foraker papers, undated.
20. *Washington Bee*, February 2, 1907, p. 1.
21. *Broad Ax*, June 20, 1908, p. 1.

22. The *Age*, December 27, 1906, p. 8.
23. *Washington Post*, November 19, 1906, p. 4.
24. U.S. *War Department Records*, Legislative files, "Brownsville."
25. *Ibid.*
26. The *Freeman*, December 22, 1906, p. 5.
27. *Washington Post*, November 30, 1906, p. 5.
28. Meier, "Negro Racial Thought in the Age of Booker T. Washington," p. 686.
29. For a discussion of the term lily-white see Paul Lewinson, *Race, Class, & Party, A History of Negro Suffrage and White Politics in the South* (New York: Russell & Russell, Inc., 1963), p. 176.
30. The *Cleveland Gazette*, February 29, 1908, p. 1.
31. The *Age*, November 22, 1906, p. 2.
32. Printed Circular Letter, July 19, 1907, signed by J. J. Richardson, Houston, Texas, Foraker papers.
33. Petition, January 16, 1907, Foraker papers.
34. Petition, from Painesville, Ohio, February 19, 1907, Foraker papers.
35. Resolutions from Colored Citizens of Wheeling, West Virginia, Foraker papers. Scott was a resident of West Virginia.
36. Statement signed by Mrs. Margaret Gregory, April 27, 1907, Foraker papers.
37. Statement signed by Gabriel L. Jones, July 27, 1907, Foraker papers.
38. Tyler to B. T. Washington, November 23, 1906, Washington papers.
39. November 7, 1906, Washington papers.
40. November 22, 1906, Washington papers.
41. December 6, 1906, Washington papers.
42. February 19, 1907, Foraker papers.
43. March 27, 1908, Washington papers.
44. Meier, "Negro Racial Thought in the Age of Booker T. Washington," p. 737.
45. August Meier, *Negro Thought in America, 1880-1915* (Ann Arbor: The University of Michigan Press, c. 1963), p. 114.
46. *Ibid.*, p. 243.
47. *Ibid.*
48. April 15, Foraker papers.
49. Mary Church Terrell, *A Colored Woman in a White World* (Washington, D.C.: Ransdell, Inc., c. 1904), chap. 27: J. T. Milholland to M. C. Terrell, September 17, 1907, Milholland papers. Quoted in Meier, *Negro Thought*, p. 240.
50. Charles Anderson to Washington, December 11, 1906, Washington papers. Quoted in Meier, *Negro Thought*, p. 240.
51. January 17, 1907, Foraker papers.
52. Anderson to Scott, February 25, 1907, Washington papers. Quoted in Meier, *Negro Thought*, p. 240.
53. Meier, *Negro Thought*, p. 173.
54. *Ibid.*, p. 174.
55. Meier, "Negro Racial Thought in the Age of Booker T. Washington," p. 485.
56. For details of the story of the Afro-American Council, see Meier, "Negro Racial Thought in the Age of Booker T. Washington," Ch. XIII, pp. 453-512.
57. Broderick papers on W. E. B. Du Bois, Schomburg Collection, N.Y.P.L.
58. W. E. B. Du Bois, "From McKinley to Wallace: My 50 Years as a Political Independent," *Masses & Mainstream* (August, 1948), 5.
59. Copy in Broderick papers on Du Bois, Niagara Movement file.
60. Quoted in the *Independent*, September 17, 1908, p. 4.

61. November 26, 1906, p. 1.
62. *Washington Post,* November 14, 1906, p. 2.
63. The *New York Times,* November 19, 1906, p. 3.
64. November 22, 1906, Washington papers.
65. November 29, 1906, p. 1.
66. The *Freeman,* June 8, 1907, p. 1.
67. The *Independent,* June 27, 1907, p. 1487.
68. March 23, 1908, Washington papers, Scrapbook, 1908.
69. *Broad Ax,* April 11, 1908, p. 1.
70. *Ibid.,* April 18, 1908, p. 3.
71. Resolutions by Shawnee County Afro-American League, April 27, 1908, Foraker papers.
72. Statement from Negro Republican League of Kansas, Foraker papers.
73. *Washington Post,* May 13, 1908, p. 4.
74. Foraker papers, no date but probably late spring or early summer, 1908.
75. Abstract of the address of Hon. Archibald H. Grimké, May 27, 1907, Foraker papers.
76. May 27, 1908, p. 6.
77. See *infra,* p. 104.
78. Printed leaflet, Foraker papers.
79. Meier, *Negro Thought,* p. 186.
80. Pamphlet issued by the National Negro American Political League, Washington, D. C., n.d., Foraker papers.
81. The *Freeman,* April 18, 1908, p. 4.
82. *Broad Ax,* June 6, 1908, p. 1.
83. Emma Lou Thornbrough, "The Brownsville Episode and the Negro Vote," *Mississippi Valley Historical Review,* XLIV (December 1957), 469-492.
84. *Washington Post,* July 27, 1908, p. 1.
85. *The Dallas Express*, quoted in the *Indianapolis World,* August 15, 1908, p. 7.
86. *Horizon,* III (Feb., 1908), 17-18; IV (Sept., 1908), 4-6.
87. Thornbrough, "The Brownsville Episode," p. 484.
88. *Ibid.*
89. *Ibid.,* p. 491.
90. *Ibid.,* p. 489-90.
91. *Ibid.,* p. 491.
92. *Ibid.,* p. 492.

VI

BOOKER T. WASHINGTON

Have we blush of shame to own them?
　Was our loyal love misplaced?
Were the Negro soldiers guilty?
　Must we feel by them disgraced?
No! We fain would wreathe fair laurels
　For those sable sons of Mars
For whom Foraker cried: "Justice!"
　Till his voice rang 'mid the stars
And we bring to this brave Saxon
　All our love, in golden bars.

Earth had mighty, dark-hued heroes
　In the morning of the World —
Giant warriors, clad in lightning,
　Who their bold defiance hurled
High as heaven and down the ages! —
　Nimrod, Seti, Rameses,
Hannibal — bold lions rampant,
　Romping thro' Dawn's amethyst —
Bronzed Nemeans, leaping, storming
　Down the Morning's amber mist!

Rise, forgotten Past! Meroe,
  Where great Moses loved, arise!
Tyre, Thebes, Nineveh, we knew you
  When the world was Paradise!
Sphinx, pyramids, and silent Momnon;
  Ruined Memphis — Babylon,
Relics of great deeds and empires
  Of the proud, dark peoples gone,
We, your clay creators, loved you
  In the clanging, purple Dawn.

Turn again to wondrous Toussaint,
  Dessalines; great Maceo;
Smalls; Dumas; or Crispus Attucks,
  Dying, Freedom's way to show
E'en to white men — Thro' rebellion's
  Blanching hells we passed again:
Pillow, Wagner, Appomatox
  Were our pray for Freedom then,
And the boom of belching cannon
  Sounded like a loud "Amen."

On that hot, barbed hill in Cuba,
  Where the Spaniards blocked the way,
At San Juan, when brave men faltered,
  Our black soldiers saved the day.
They were men like Mingo Sanders,
  Heroes of the camp and fight.
Were they cowards down in Brownsville?
  Dread marayders of the night?
Veterans bathed in holy battle,
  Where dark Lethe rolled in sight!

Who are these dark people, Saxons,
  Dwelling 'mongst you, humbled so?
Children of the warrior nations
  Whom Omnipotence brought low.
God, the Alpha and Omega,
  Brings the boasters still to naught.
Blest, O blessed are the meek ones
  Who His sable robes have caught!
Hark! The ancients whisper thro' us
  To the Present, mystery-fraught.[1]

In recent years many scholars have reevaluated Booker T. Washington's
role and have appraised it, on balance, positively. August Meier's interpreta-

tion is representative:

> Although overtly Washington minimized the importance of the franchise
> and civil rights, he was deeply involved in political affairs and in efforts
> to prevent disfranchisement and other forms of discrimination.[2]

Thus, in spite of Washington's accommodating tone and his verbal emphasis
upon economy as the solution to the race problem, this scholar wrote:

> Washington was surreptitiously engaged in undermining the American
> race system. . . .and in spite of his strictures against political activity, he
> was a powerful politician in his own right.[3]

Despite activity he was engaged in surreptitiously, Washington's major
impact and influence were felt publicly, and in the Brownsville case, at least,
his surreptitious activity did not run counter to his public stance but rein-
forced it.

While the black community as a whole was actively protesting the President's action, "Washington, the best-known and most influential American
Negro, was noticeably silent."[4] Roosevelt's Brownsville policy placed Washington in an embarrassing and precarious position, for it threatened his
prestige and influence as a leader in the black community. Influential as
Washington was, Brownsville was an issue on which he could not successfully
silence dissent. In spite of his efforts to suppress criticism of Roosevelt and
later Taft through pressure exerted upon newspapers, individuals and organizations, opposition to the Administration grew and much spilled over to
include Washington.

Washington's public attitude toward agitation is well known. Two statements issued by him during the Brownsville controversy and in the wake of
the Atlanta riot, which occurred shortly after the troop discharge order, sum
up his stated policy:

> Let us not become unduly alarmed or depressed when seasons of distur-
> bance and riot overtake us. . . . Has anything occurred in recent years
> that will begin to compare with the horrors of the trials of reconstruc-
> tion. . . . Every iota of influence that we possess should be used to get
> rid of the criminal and loafing element of our people. . . . While con-
> demning the giving of prominence to the work of mobs in the South, we
> should not fail to give due credit to those of the white race who have
> stood manfully and courageously on the side of law and order.

The following year Washington addressed the Jamestown Exposition and said,
in part:

> In nine-tenths of our Southern communities there is peace and harmony,
> good will and friendship; but when one goes outside of the Southern
> states, when one goes into the North, into Europe as I have done, and

reads the dispatches that come from the South, it is always one thing –
lynchings. And you never hear of any other news from the South except
lynchings. Those people naturally get the idea, other people get the idea,
through this unusual punishment, that we are living in a state of turmoil, '
at daggers points throughout the South, whereas, as a matter of fact, as
you go through the average Southern community you will find a feeling
of mutual confidence, a feeling of friendship existing between the races
– each race interested in the progress of the other.[5]

Roosevelt replied to a request from Washington to reconsider the discharge order as follows:

I could not possibly refrain from acting as regard these colored soldiers.
You cannot have any information to give me privately to which I could
pay heed, my dear Mr. Washington, because the information on which I
act is that which came out of the investigation itself.[6]

Unable to convince the President, who thereupon had business out of the
country, Washington urged Secretary of War Taft not to execute the order
until Roosevelt's return, obviously hoping to have success when the question
was reopened. Taft did temporarily suspend the order until he received a
vigorous response from Roosevelt to go ahead. "When Roosevelt returned in
November, Washington sent Scott and Anderson to the White House with a
message. The contents of the message were not revealed, but whatever they
were they did not cause the President to modify his stand."[7]

Washington's position, which he expanded upon in letters to friends in
the months that followed, was that his disagreements with the President must
remain private. ". . .the enemy will, as usual, try to blame me for all this.
They can talk; I cannot, without being disloyal to our friend, who I mean to
stand by throughout his administration," said Washington to a confidante.[8]
Roosevelt was often referred to in private correspondence as "our friend,"
the opposition of the moment as "the enemy."

Early in 1907 the Cleveland *Leader* asked Washington for a statement
concerning the abuse directed at Roosevelt on Brownsville. In reply he reiterated the statement he had previously made at a banquet in Charleston, West
Virginia:

We cannot expect to win our battles in the South or North by a policy
of antagonism. Civilization soon tires of a race, as of an individual, that
continually whines or complains. And, likewise, the country will not
tolerate any element in the population abusing and cursing the chief
executive.[9]

This statement was reprinted widely in the Negro press.

The *Echo*, a black newspaper from Alpena, Michigan, reprinted a letter
of Washington's in which he defended Roosevelt on the grounds that black

troops should be no more immune from punishment than white soldiers. Although he admitted that there were many instances where white troops also should have been, but were not, "discharged for riotous act, all respectable and law-abiding colored people of the country are behind the President in his discharge of the three companies," said Washington.[10]

Washington, in an effort to offset criticism, privately circulated information that he had tried to deter the President. To Ralph Tyler he wrote that he did his best to dissuade Roosevelt from taking the action he did, but the President seemed to feel that under the circumstances he could not refrain from acting as he had. "I feel sure, however," Washington went on, "that gradually he will reinstate all the men who had no knowledge of the outbreak."

> In the meantime it is a fact, as you state, that the matter had stirred up the Negro to a very high pitch of agitation. . . . I agree with you thoroughly that there is a danger now that the race will get a setback among its friends in the North by these intemperate utterances and frequent indignation meetings. Of course, it was natural that some protest should be made, but I fear there is danger of too much of it. One thing the American people will not stand for any length of time, and this is abuse of any group of people of the President of the United States, and if our people make the mistake of going too far, there will be a reaction in the North among the people and newspapers who have stood by us. I am doing all I can to check the folly. I am writing Mr. Fortune on the subject to-day.[11]

In the many communications to friends and associates defending his private efforts in behalf of the soldiers, Washington closed with the request to maintain the confidential nature of the letter. To some he wrote simply that, and then enclosed a copy of Roosevelt's statement to him. Such an unadorned explanation went to Whitefield McKinley noted "Personal and Confidential"; a similar letter went to Reverend James H. Gordon, also marked "Personal."[12]

To Oswald Garrison Villard, who had a long history of dissent, the tone was appropriately more militant.

> I did my full duty in trying to persuade him from the course not only when I saw him, but wrote to him strongly after reaching New York. I am not going to give up. . . .There is no law, human or divine, which justified the punishment of an innocent man. I have the strongest faith in the President's honest. . .high mindedness. . .sincere unselfishness and courage, but I regret for all these reasons all the more this thing has occurred.[13]

Villard was hardly pacified by Washington's efforts or explanation, for he responded by describing Roosevelt "as the shifting sands," and "the worst President we have had in 25 years."[14]

To F. J. Garrison, Washington gave assurances that "the President will take up the matter and gradually restore a large number of individuals to the battalion. I do not believe that he will permit the matter to rest where it is."[15]

To some others he intimated or stated outright that the President's action was based upon inside information, despite Roosevelt's clear statement to the contrary. To Bishop Grant, for instance, he wrote that he was sorry indeed, as he had told him, that Roosevelt thought it necessary to take the action he did regarding the three colored companies. "Of course, he has gone inside the facts which he has not given to the public which he claims justifies his action."[16] To Bishop Grant, naturally, he did not enclose a copy of Roosevelt's statement, in which he dispels any notion of inside facts.

To another loyal and conservative ally, S. Laing Williams, Washington had a slightly different approach. In a letter, the direct business of which was to discuss an appointment Williams was seeking from Roosevelt through Washington, Washington again described his efforts at dissuading the President from carrying out the discharge.[17] A few days later, in another letter, Washington referred to Roosevelt's actions as a "great mistake" but wrote of the "growing under-current in many of the Northern papers" to the effect that "he has reasons which he has not made public."[18] By December Washington was more disturbed by the protests against the dismissals than by the dismissals. Again to Williams he wrote:

> I very much fear that these frequent meetings held by these agitators are hurting us tremendously in the North, in fact I am sure they are. There are many sections of the North where the Negro as an individual or as a race is not thought of separate from the other portion of American citizenship except when the attention of white people is called to it through these meetings. If our people would have a meeting once in a while for the purpose of starting a bank, insurance company or building a railroad or opening a coal mine, it would be far different, but practically every time the white man hears from the Negro in an organized capacity it is in connection with a meeting of condemnation or protest. I do not say that we hold them so often that they grow monotonous, tiresome and hurtful to a large class of people in the North. The sentiment of the white people in Boston has almost been completely changed within a few months by reason of this senseless agitation.[19]

While the agitation raged publicly, Washington was making efforts privately to repair the damage done by the discharge of the troops. Early in the Brownsville agitation, Washington wrote to Taft asking if the War Department intended to enlist additional black soldiers to take the place of those who were dismissed. In an early draft the following sentence, later dropped, appeared: "I cannot tell you how deeply the colored people feel about the dismissal of these companies."[20] Taft responded promptly that it was indeed the intention of the War Department to enlist additional colored soldiers at once.

Again Washington wrote to Taft asking whether it was legal for any state to refuse to give blacks any recognition in the state militia and still draw its quota from the public fund toward the support of the state militia. He pointed out that several of the southern states had recently mustered out all of the colored companies.[21] Taft replied that "it was beyond the power of the United States Government to prescribe the composition of regiments or companies of the organized militia in time of peace, a function which is expressly vested in the states by the Federal Government. If it could be shown, however, that the state authorities had acted arbitrarily then it might be possible to reduce the allotment."[22]

Emmett Scott became concerned at this time with Negro musicians in the army. Years before, he wrote to Taft, white men were appointed chief musicians in charge of black regimental army bands because "at that time there were no capable colored musicians available." The custom was still in force, Scott said, "although the cause had long since ceased to exist. The enlistment of white men for the position of chief musician in Negro bands closed the door of opportunity and promotion to the best black talent in the service and made it harder to enlist desirable colored musicians."[23] Taft replied promptly with a most revealing comment that Roosevelt "seems favorably inclined. . .but before deciding definitely prefers to see the character of the report on the Brownsville affair."[24]

In an effort to end the agitation on the Brownsville issue, Washington exerted his influence in a variety of ways. The most direct was by the straightforward use of his prestige and power. For example, he "offered a suggestion" to William Ashley Taliaferro, pastor of the First Baptist Church in Opelika, Alabama, "in the best of spirit." "It strikes me," Washington wrote, "if you can find it in your heart to do so, that at this particular time" it would be opportune for him, as a leader, to issue a public statement upholding the President in his actions in regard to the Brownsville affair. Surely Roosevelt would have done the same had the soldiers been white, Washington assured him, for "he has always been a friend of the negro, as you well know." Washington concluded by saying that he simply made the suggestion as "I believe it to be wise and helpful for the future."[25] Such a letter was not uncommon.

Washington's correspondence is also filled with communications from his closest associates who reported regularly on the political situation. During the Brownsville period such reporting meant information on pro-Foraker meetings, who attended such meetings, and who said what. Washington's nephew, Albert Johnston, employed by the Internal Revenue Service in Birmingham, was, for instance, a regular correspondent. Charles Anderson also reported regularly on any anti-Washington activities.

Washington could be ruthless with those he identified as his enemy, in this case, those who spoke out against the Administration's policy on Brownsville. To George Cortelyou of the United States Post Office in Washington he wrote that the man "who is more responsible than all the others put together for stirring up trouble against the administration on the Brownsville affair, draws the money which he is using in this fight from your department." Washington added that but for his work and expenditure of money "which he gets from the Post Office Department, the whole Brownsville affair would have been almost forgotten before this time," and that he had paid for the speakers' fees and the halls in which the protest meetings had been held. Washington conceded that "he has not appeared personally at any of these meetings but I could give you indisputable evidence" that he was behind it all. Pinned to the covering letter is a scribbled addition:

> This man is practically all there is to the Constitutional League. He uses that name to hide his own personal identity.[26]

Later the same year Anderson informed Washington that a letter printed in the *Guardian* "he felt confident" came from Bruce Grit. The letter stated that T. T. Fortune had made Washington famous and had been repaid by being fired from the newspaper he spent a lifetime building up simply because he refused to support Roosevelt and Taft on Brownsville. Anderson advised Washington that the presumed author of the letter works for General Clarkson in the Administration and that his employment there should be called to the attention of "our friend" so that immediate action could be taken. Nothing should transpire by letter, he cautioned, because it would be forwarded to Clarkson.[27]

Anderson continued to inform Washington of the government employment of those who spoke out against the Administration on Brownsville. Again he wrote to Washington that he informed "our friend" that it was time something was done against those who inspired "these newspaper attacks" and further, that the man in the Interior Department was the leading spirit. He had suggested at least a reduction in rank or a transfer. Roosevelt had turned the letter over to Secretary Garfield, who was concerned as to the accuracy of the charge. Anderson was thus writing to Washington to ask him to write to Garfield and identify "this particular man as the head devil." "Let us urge immediate and drastic action in this matter now," Anderson concluded, "while they are in the humor to meet our wishes."[28]

Washington and his associates had an ambiguous relationship with Gilchrist Stewart. Whitefield McKinley wrote to his chief that Stewart was there in Washington, "but I think we have succeeded in keeping him from making a fool of himself" by lending himself to Foraker and Humphrey, although he did blunder in sending the petition to Congress before first letting the President pass on it.[29] A few days later Stewart wrote a lengthy and stiffly respectful letter to Washington thanking him for the "moral support you have given me — sub rosa — in my fight to have justice done" to the discharged soldiers. He urged Washington to examine the Constitution League's evidence and, if impressed, to request Roosevelt to offer remedial legislation and thereby preclude a Congressional fight. "Will you not make a perusal of my evidence," he asked, "and bring this view of the situation to the President?"

Further on in his letter, Stewart discussed the rumor that Washington and Anderson "desired my elimination as an important political factor here in New York State." Of course he did not believe such reports, because "ever since you ... effected a reconciliation between Mr. Anderson and myself I, of course, have thought that I always could depend upon your friendship and have also pulled true with Mr. Anderson." His postscript was: "my activity in the Constitution League is a desire to benefit the race. . . . I am not attacking any person or persons."[30] Washington's reply, if he replied, is not available.

Anderson wrote to Washington shortly after advising him of the Constitution League's difficult financial situation, information received from Solomon Johnson who was also able to provide details concerning telephone conversations between Stewart and Milholland. Other information included a meeting in Wetmore's office which Bishop Walters and three or four others attended. "I saw them entering the building, and saw them in the office for over an hour. I can stand in Nassau Street and look into Wetmore's office easily."[31] To Scott, Anderson wrote of Stewart: "I hope you will remember this scoundrel when the time comes to stick in the knife."[32] And again to Scott, Anderson advised that Washington cease meeting with the Constitution League people, because they know every move the Doctor makes. It is always dangerous business to deal with men who are playing two ways, Anderson advised. "If you want to win a battle, you had better confer only with your officers and keep your plans unknown to the enemy," Anderson suggested. Scott replied that Washington wished more specific information, that he had just met with Stewart but was "careful not to say anything informative."[33]

Roosevelt, with the advice and support of Washington, used patronage appointments to consolidate his position in the Brownsville struggle. The most famous incident involved the effort to appoint Ralph W. Tyler as surveyor of the port of Cincinnati, Foraker's home city. The details of that appointment have been described elsewhere.[34] The appointment was ultimately not made because of the opposition by many white Republicans in Ohio, including Roosevelt's son-in-law, Nicholas Longworth. Instead, Tyler was appointed to the less visible post of auditor in the Navy Department in Washington, D.C., where "it was hoped, he would be useful in keeping Negroes faithful to the Republican party."[35]

The political implications of the intended appointment of Tyler were widely known.

The Columbus, Ohio *Press* stated that even the most ardent Administration politicians admitted that the appointment of Ralph Tyler was the result of the Brownsville investigation. "Mr. Tyler would never have been heard of if it had not been for the desire of President Roosevelt to punish Senator Foraker."[36]

Many of the black newspapers were openly scornful of Tyler's nomination. Before the appointment was made the *Cleveland Gazette* remarked:

> There ought not to be, and we trust there is not, a member of the race in Ohio so ungrateful and disloyal as to permit himself to be used by the President of the United States or any other person as a club with which to "punish" politically the most aggressive and best friend of the race in America today – Senator Foraker – for his efforts in behalf of the race.[37]

An editorial writer for the influential *Washington Bee* declared that if he, the writer, were Ralph Tyler, he would inform the President "that I object to being used as a catspaw or toady to rebuke a man who has been a friend to my race." Such an appointment, the newspaper claimed, "will influence only one in the entire state of Ohio, and that vote is no doubt doubtful – Ralph W. Tyler."[38]

Washington's public response to the Tyler affair was politically wise if somewhat less than candid. Washington enthusiastically defended the appointment and used the occasion to attack Foraker, who, he said, has had ample opportunity during his career to name some Negro to an important position and had not done so. "The fact that the President's consideration of a colored man exposes the hypocrisy of his pretended friendship is only too evident."[39]

Washington's other major effort to minimize rebellion was directed at the press. The overwhelming majority of newspapers supported Washington's policies in general, partly because of his persuasive powers and partly because they shared his views. Washington admitted that he worked to cultivate "in a general and friendly way" almost all of the Negro editors and leaders.[40] His correspondence provides much evidence of his profound influence over the press and substantiates the charges made during his lifetime that he secretly subsidized newspapers and magazines.

Washington worked through R. W. Thompson's National Negro Press Bureau in Washington, a valuable ally, for Thompson provided news and information for many of the smaller Negro papers. Washington's correspondence leaves no doubt that Thompson was a devoted Washington supporter, for their letters back and forth contained such information as which newspapers were "safe," what kinds of pressures could be safely used on which papers, and which stories would best aid the Republicans in the campaign. For example, in a letter to Washington during the Taft campaign, Thompson wrote of having given Mr. Oulahan, a Republican party representative, a list of "preferred papers." Mr. Oulahan also gave him some "instructions." "News matter calculated to show Taft's popularity with the colored people is to be played up strong; the Republican party's record on the Negro rights to be boosted, with criticism of the Democracy's restricted; Brownsville and 'Its champion' to be ignored as far as possible; not too much stress on emancipation and the past, but bear on the present-day reasons for preferring the Republican party."[41]

August Meier has described in detail the variety of methods Washington utilized.[42] By wide use of Tuskegee news releases and advertisements, his influence was felt. Several journals, at least five, were "aided by sustained cash contributions."[43] These were the *Age, The Washington Colored American, The Boston Colored Citizen, Alexander's Magazine* and *The Colored American.* These newspapers, as Meier demonstrates, were well selected. The *Age*, edited by Fortune, was the leading black newspaper. The Boston and Washington newspapers competed with leading critics of Washington's, Trotter's *Guardian* in Boston and Calvin Chase's *Bee* in Washington.

Fortune had at one time been a close friend and supporter of Washington but he remained unpredictable on the Brownsville matter, although by the beginning of 1907, as the election loomed, Fortune was succumbing to pressure. (To keep close touch with the *Age's* office, Scott was in frequent correspondence with E. T. Atwell from the staff. In one communication to Scott, Atwell complained that Fortune refused to take suggestions, really believing that he ran his own paper.)[44]

If Fortune appeared to lessen his hostility to Roosevelt as the presidential elections drew near, Grimké, who ran a regular by-line column, did not. In one of his many articles on the Brownsville case, Grimké wrote:

> In this posture of the contending forces, we regret exceedingly the wholly selfish use which the President is making of Mr. Washington and the colored people in his battle for political successorship with Senator Foraker and the powerful interests and classes which he is leading. Neither Washington nor the colored people can risk the hazard to be moved as a mere pawn on this chess board of the President. If Roosevelt must consult Washington in such matters then the conference ought to be regarded as strictly confidential, and Washington's name and the counsels or suggestions made by him ought not to be given to the press by the President. For while publicity in such a case may serve the President's purpose or scheme, it does not serve those of Washington,

but instead operate to his hurt, to the hurt of Tuskegee and to the great cause of the race in America for long years to come.[45]

Washington was very much concerned about Grimké's weekly column and wrote to Fortune of his grievances:

It seems that the influence of the paper will become weakened by so much abuse and criticism of the President, and I am of the opinion that it would be much better and exert a more satisfactory influence for good if his columns treated of matters along conservative lines.

Fortune complied within a week.

I have turned down Grimké's article today, as it is a rehash of Brownsville, and told him he would have to treat the President and Secretary Taft in a more dignified way. I know he will get his back up, but if he does not like it I will have to cut him out.[46]

Such compliance evidently did not suffice, for when Washington purchased the paper later that year he replaced Fortune with Fred R. Moore. Moore took charge of the paper with the issue of October 3, 1907. "Ralph W. Tyler wrote the 'Brownsville Ghouls' editorial for the issue of October 17 which marked the reversal of the *Age's* Brownsville policy."[47]

The "Brownsville Ghouls" editorial condemned those who

crouching behind avarice and selfishness, were ready to swoop down, buzzard-like, upon the prey. When Senator Foraker . . . specifically stated in the onset that "it is not a question of race or color, but a question as to the right of the President to discharge troops in time of peace," these human ghouls raised the black flag of Race Discrimination and moved out in search, not of justice, but the thirty pieces of silver coined for Judases . . . this vagabond of parasites marched up and down flaunting the color question that they might receive the thirty pieces.

Washington expressed his opinion of Moore in a letter to Charles Alexander of *Alexander's Magazine.* "Mr. Moore is nothing but a messenger boy and hardly deserves serious attention." Whose messenger boy he is is clear from the Washington-Moore correspondence. "All of the letters on *Age* stationary are now ready. Shall we forward them to Mr. Moore for him to sign and mail them out from New York City?" wrote Scott to Washington.[48]

Washington's letters to Moore are filled with orders concerning editorial and news matters. Washington even complained to Moore that his office was sloppy and advised him to clean it up. Scott too addressed him brusquely: "You remember our understanding to the effect that you were to send out monthly statements of the amount of business done by the *Age*. To date I have not received a statement covering either January or February."[49] At one point Washington admonished Moore for using the word "lie" several times in the editorial. It cheapens the paper, he said. He also objected to the excessive use of Trotter's name and the name of his opponent's newspaper as it provided free advertising.

Washington and Tyler regularly contributed, not just ideas for editorials, but the written editorials. Washington, according to one letter, sent Moore two editorials to run in the *Age:* one, "A Plain Duty in Every Community"; the other, a short pro-Taft one on "lily-whites" in the South. Tyler, too, was journalistically active. In a letter to Scott he referred to Fortune's letter in a previous *Guardian,* which he answered in a short editorial under the caption "Dementia-Americana." "It is written for a three-fold purpose," he explained: "to deny the charge of ownership; to rebuke Trotter for taking advantage of Fortune's tottering mind . . .; and to warn the public that anything from Fortune can be charged up to a mind that is lost."[50] August Meier's description of Tyler as a venal politician appears apt.

On October 31 Tyler wrote to Scott: "Next week's editorial contributions will consist of the following . . . ." including a constitutional defense of Roosevelt. On November 8 he again wrote to Scott: "My editorial contributions for next week include the following . . . ."[52]

Tyler's "Brownsville Ghouls" editorial created complications which were not immediately recognized. Moore wrote to Scott happily informing him that "Mr. Tyler is giving splendid assistance. His ed on 'The Brownsville Ghouls' is I think a corker – am sending marked copies to all the leading papers in the country."[53] Scott wrote to Tyler promptly that his editorial matter "which you have outlined for the *Age* will be altogether satisfactory, I am sure. The Brownsville Ghouls article was especially fine." He then advised him not to send too much pro-Taft or pro-Roosevelt matter. Moore is "all right as regards both of them," but "I am inclined to agree with the opinion of the Doctor" that because of the postion taken by the *Age* under Fortune "it might be well gradually to work up, say by December or January, instead of at this particular time, the pro-Taft position."[54]

Scott then wrote to Moore some days later sending letters he received from Tyler and Washington's answer. "He most likely will be sending you this editorial very soon, and if so, it has occurred to me that you ought to send him a reply about as the one herewith attached. You can rewrite it on your paper. You must not by any means permit him to interfere with the matter, which you are already having put through." Attached was a copy of the following letter written by Washington to Tyler on November 2, 1907.

> I have written Mr. Moore. . . . my frank opinion that as I now notice it, the editorial on Brownsville Ghouls has proved a boomerang, as it has too quickly, after his taking charge of the paper, following his purchase of Fortune's interest, suddenly changed its attitude.

Note how carefully Washington refers to Moore's taking charge of the paper after Moore's purchase of Fortune's interest. Washington was concerned lest he be known as the owner of the *Age* "I am not sorry that you have forgotten the editorial note in which my name is also used. I am quite sure it is wiser to keep my name out of your paper for a good while."[55] Despite such precautions the insinuations persisted that Washington did, as indeed he did, own and control the *Age*. Thus as Scott wrote to Moore:

> the more our friend thinks of the matter, the more decided he is in the opinion that he ought absolutely to withdraw from any connection whatever with the property. He wants you to take over so that he will be in position absolutely to declare that he has no real relations with the property. To this end, he has asked me to draw twenty-six notes for $500 each covering the following items . . . .

Some days later Moore responded: "I signed notes and returned them to you . . . . Stock has been turned over to me and now every thing is ok. The damn niggers can now say what they please. Best thing to do is to retain a stiff upper lip."[56]

An examination of the leading newspapers and magazines indicates that while Washington's influence over the black press was significant, he was unable to control the activity of most of them to his satisfaction, and that it was the Brownsville position which most of them were unwilling to accept. Washington did not stop trying. To George W. Cable of the *Freeman* he wrote:

> I very much fear that our people will over-do the matter of condemnation of the President and the holding of indignation meetings. I think so far, the best public sentiment of the country has been with us, but if we go too far in the matter of abusing the President of the United States there will be a tremendous reaction, and I am wondering if you cannot make such a suggestion in your paper in some form.[57]

Two years later Washington was still interested in the *Freeman*. He received a report from Thompson that a representative from the paper was in New York and "it seems that a satisfactory arrangement has been made and the paper will wheel into line. Knox has been playing for an advance from the committee and has had Lewis under instructions to say nothing definite as to the political attitude of the editorial page . . . . The Bee, Age, Reformer, Cleveland Journal, Charleston Advocate, Florida Sentinel, Long Branch (N.J.) Echo and a few others are giving very satisfactory service."[58]

Charles Alexander had only praise for "the man who subsidized him."[59] In the summer of 1907 he was still writing such loyal notes to Washington as the following:

> Have you seen Trotter's paper lately? Trotter has been publishing some

very hard lies about you of late. He ought to have his wings clipped. I would like to do the job. I think of starting a weekly soon for the purpose of ripping him up the back. Will have the co-operation of quite a number of fine fellows. Will write again soon about this matter.[60]

But on the Brownsville matter even Alexander was difficult to move. In late 1907 and into 1908 he continued to criticize Taft for his Brownsville stand. In 1908 he went so far as to suggest that blacks, as a balance of power, might consider voting for the Democrats. Washington was furious with him.[61] By the end of August, though, Washington had persuaded Alexander, for he endorsed Taft.

If the Brownsville episode made defense of Roosevelt difficult for Washington, Roosevelt's annual message in 1906 put another severe strain upon Washington's agility and imagination. The message was issued in the midst of the Brownsville controversy and it was carefully examined by many black leaders. Several sentences in the message aroused great concern. For example:

> The greatest existing cause of lynching is the perpetration, especially by black men, of the hideous crime of rape.

And later,

> The white people of the South indict the whole colored race on the ground that even the better elements lend no assistance whatever in ferreting out criminals of their own color. The respectable colored people must learn not to harbor their criminals, but to assist the officers in bringing them to justice. This is the larger crime, and it provokes such atrocious offenses as the one at Atlanta.

And again,

> Every colored man should realize that the worst enemy of his race is the negro criminal, and above all the negro criminal who commits the dreadful crime of rape; and it should be felt as in the highest degree an offense against the whole country, and against the colored race in particular, for a colored man to fail to help the officers of the law in hunting down with all possible earnestness and zeal every such offender.[62]

Washington found himself trapped into explaining and apologizing for Roosevelt, because the previous October, two months before the message was delivered, Washington had been called to the capital to consult with Roosevelt on it. "I am planning to be in Washington within a few days to see our friend there, who has asked me to see him regarding some matters," Washington wrote to Whitefield McKinley.[63] And again to him a few days later: "This is for your own eyes and must not get out. The President is planning to take up the Southern riots in his message to Congress. I am to see him about the matter soon."[64] To Oswald Garrison Villard he expressed the hope that.

"he will be able to say something that will help the situation though it will be a difficult task."[65]

After Washington met with Roosevelt his optimism waned.

> I spent over an hour with the President in taking up in detail his message. He did not take all the medicine which we prescribed for him, but he did take a portion of it. He agreed to modify most of the objectionable expressions except those in the first paragraph; when I tackled him on that, he gritted his teeth and absolutely refused to budge a single inch. He did, however, preface what he had originally written with another introduction which will soften the first part of the message somewhat.[66]

Shortly after, Kelly Miller, a sometime supporter of Washington's, wrote him expressing regret that Roosevelt refused to modify the first part of his statement which "tends to blacken the reputation of the whole race. I could wish that he had preserved an unbroken silence rather than help to confirm the world in the growing belief that the Negro is by nature of a lecherous disposition. However, there is no doubt that your intervention helped to relieve the severity of his utterance, if it could not make it altogether acceptable."[67]

Miller had second thoughts less than a week later and wrote again to Washington that

> the more I think of it the more I am convinced of the lasting hurt that this utterance will do the race. The Negro is held up as a race of criminals and rapists, banded together to uphold one another in crime, with only occasional individual exceptions. No further justification would be needed by those who despitefully treat us. This utterance from the White House will do more to damn the Negro to everlasting infamy than all the maledictions of Tillman, Vardaman, Dixon and John Temple Graves. . . .The Negro will be branded as a lecherous race, with the authority of the President of the United States. . . . The President's recent order dismissing the colored battalion has evoked the universal condemnation of the race. If upon the heels of this action he sends out this damaging statement, it will surely aggravate the bitter feeling already engendered. . . .In the minds of many you are held responsible for the dismissal of the colored soldiers, although few fair minded men could believe that you counselled it. You will allow Mr. Roosevelt to do you a great wrong if he sends forth this reproach against the Negro race. Pardon me for writing so freely. I deeply appreciate the gravity of the situation.[68]

The substance of the letter and its author were not such as to be ignored by Washington. His response was prompt.

Of course, all of us could have discussed the President's Message in a little different light if we had had any idea of his intended action regarding the Negro troops. He did not mention the matter to me until I saw him that evening, and then he told me that the matter had been decided. I tried to persuade him to take a different course but without success . . . . I do not believe that the general effect of his message on rape and lynching is going to be as bad as you now fear it will . . . . The great mass of people whom the Message is sought to reach and influence will simply, in my opinion, get the general effect of it, which is that he condemned crime of all character among all races. I think that is the sum total of what the President is trying to say, and I believe that will be the impression left upon the average man . . . . you must bear in mind that he has for his object the saying of something that will help to make life and property for the Negro in the South safer, and in order to do this he has, in a measure, placed himself in touch with the Southern people. I am now simply presenting his case . . . . there are certain features of it which I wish might have been changed, especially the first part of it. I wish also that he had modified more than he did the part . . . where he speaks about Negroes hunting down criminals, and also a little more the part where he refers to speedy trials . . . . The President or no one else has ever asked me to be his official advisor in regard to race matters. All matters outside of my immediate educational work, especially anything that bears upon politics is exceedingly distasteful to me.[69]

Fortune was less moderate in his criticism, both of Roosevelt's message and of Washington's role in preparing it.

I am sorry that the President did not let you blue pencil his message, as far as it relates to us, and all the more so as he has employed throughout the message your phraseology and often your idioms. His advice that Afro-Americans who know nothing of their criminals shall help to hunt them down and his adoption of the lynch law method of slaying the innocent with the guilty are vile propositions calculated to do us great injury . . . .

The President has forfeited the confidence and good esteem of the Afro-American people and largely of the American people by the adoption of Southern ideas and methods . . . . He has two years more as President, and you have the remainder of your life as the controlling genius of the Tuskegee Institute and leader of the Afro-American people, and your future will depend largely on how far you allow it to be understood that you sponsor what he says and does as far as the Afro-American people are concerned.[70]

To certain correspondents Washington was considerably less critical of the tone and substance of Roosevelt's message. He wrote an unsolicited letter to Theodore W. Jones in response to a letter by him in the *Chicago Conservator*. "There is no doubt about it," Washington wrote him, "the criminality of our race is greatly injuring our standing before the American people, but this is much more marked in some sections of the North than in the South. We will gain nothing by not seeing their conditions frankly and squarely."[71]

Washington was shrewd enough to understand that whatever the intensity of anger and outrage among Afro-Americans, what mattered was whether these feelings were reflected in voting behavior. Let the black community howl, but just let it continue to vote Republican. As early as September, 1907, Washington had his attention directed to the coming presidential election. In a communication to Roosevelt he described the National Negro Baptist Convention, with some 3,000 delegates, as "feeling toward you and your administration kindly" with the exception of a few extreme radicals. A resolution condemning the Administration's course on Brownsville failed. The feeling indicated at this convention, he went on, "I think is representative of the change that is taking place gradually among our people in most parts of the country."[72] Later in the year he wrote again to Roosevelt, this time from Boston, where, as discussed earlier, the Brownsville matter proved to have no serious influence in alienating the black vote from the Republicans, partly because of the activities in which Washington was engaged while there.

Washington, in a letter to Taft, explained that blacks are naturally Republicans and "our hope lies in following our natural inclinations. I believe the negro vote will go largely to Secretary Taft."[73]

Washington was right.

NOTES

1. By Rev. James D. Corrothers, in published pamphlet, *To Joseph B. Foraker,* 1909, on occasion of presentation to Foraker by the Colored Citizens of Washington, D.C. at Metropolitan A.M.E. Church, March 6, 1909, of a silver loving cup.
2. Meier, *Negro Thought,* p. 110.
3. *Ibid.,* p. 114.
4. Thornbrough, "The Brownsville Affair," p. 473.
5. *The Neuse River Times,* November 22, 1906, p. 1, Washington papers, Scrapbook, 1906-07; August 3, 1907, Washington papers, Addresses, 1903-10.
6. November 5, 1906, Washington papers. Also quoted in Thornbrough, "The Brownsville Affair," p. 474.
7. Thornbrough, "The Brownsville Affair," p. 475.
8. November 7, 1906, Washington papers. Also quoted in Thornbrough, "The Brownsville Affair," p. 475.
9. Reprinted in the Urbana, Ohio *Citizen,* January 23, 1907, Washington papers, Scrapbook, 1906-07.
10. January 16, 1907, Washington papers, Scrapbook, 1907.

11. November 7, 1906, Washington papers.
12. November 7, 1906 and December 3, 1906, Washington papers.
13. November 10, 1906, Washington papers.
14. November 16, 1906, Washington papers.
15. November 5, 1906, Washington papers.
16. November 19, 1906, Washington papers.
17. November 9, 1906, Washington papers.
18. November 13, 1906, Washington papers.
19. December 3, 1906, Washington papers.
20. November 20, 1906, Washington papers.
21. Undated letter, Washington papers.
22. March 10, 1908, Washington papers.
23. December 12, 1908, Washington papers.
24. February 5, 1909, Washington papers.
25. December 13, 1906, Washington papers.
26. January 28, 1907, Washington papers.
27. October 21, 1907, Washington papers.
28. May 27, 1907, Washington papers.
29. December 13,1906, Washington papers.
30. December 17, 1906, Washington papers.
31. January 8, 1907, Washington papers.
32. January 30, 1907, Washington papers.
33. February 15, 1908 and February 26, 1908, Washington papers.
34. Thornbrough, "The Brownsville Episode."
35. *Ibid.*, p. 479.
36. April 14, 1907, Washington papers.
.37. February 9, 1907, p. 1.
38. April 20, 1907, p. 3.
39. Washington papers, undated, 1908 Correspondence.
40. Washington to Garrison, May 17, 1905, Washington papers.
41. October 7, 1908, Washington papers.
42. Meier, *Negro Thought,* pp. 225 ff.
43. *Ibid.* p. 225.
44. February 1, 1907, Washington papers.
45. February 14, 1907, p. 1.
46. Washington to Fortune, April 8, 1907; Fortune to Washington, April 15, 1907, Washington papers.
47. Meier, *Negro Thought,* p. 229.
48. October 30, 1908, Washington papers.
49. March 7, 1908, Washington papers.
50. November 20, 1907, Washington papers.
51. Meier, *Negro Thought*, p. 252.
52. November 8, 1907, Washington papers.
53. October 12, 1907, Washington papers.
54. October 13, 1907, Washington papers.
55. October 21, 1907, Washington papers.
56. November 23, 1907, Washington papers.
57. December 4, 1906, Washington papers.
58. October 3, 1908, Washington papers.
59. Meier, "Negro Racial Thought in the Age of Booker T. Washington," p. 662.

60. July 26, 1907, Washington papers.
61. Washington to Anderson, August 10, 1908, Washington papers.
62. James D. Richardson, ed., *A Compilation of the Messages and Papers of the Presidents, 1789-1908* (New York: Bureau of National Literature and Art, 1909), XV, December 3, 1906, 7030-33.
63. October 22, 1906, Washington papers.
64. October 25, 1906, Washington papers.
65. October 28, 1906, Washington papers.
66. Washington to McKinley, November 8, 1906, Washington papers.
67. November 10, 1906, Washington papers.
68. November 16, 1906, Washington papers.
69. November 19, 1906, Washington papers.
70. December 8, 1906, Washington papers.
71. November 14, 1906, Washington papers.
72. September 19, 1907, Washington papers.
73. October 7, 1908, Washington papers.

VII

THE BLACK PRESS

Hans on the Black Soldiers

Say, Meester President Roosevelt
  Vas dit Von Purdy get
Is dot Southern Texas town
  About dose soldiers yet.

One time you vas der square deal man,
  Und makes fine dot speech
Meine frau die Katheren say
  Hans, dot man is er peach. . . .

I at Sedan spill mein bloot
  So freely like er sprink
I starve und sleep upon mein arms,
  But dot vas leetle didink. . . .

But ven you tread upon so hard,
  Poor soldiers such as I,
I take again die wooden shoes,
  Und told dis land good-bye.[1]

"For once, a brief, but glorious once, the colored press, pulpit and people were united," wrote the fiery F. H. M. Murray of the Brownsville case.[2] The black press reflected well not only the glorious unity but its brief quality as well.

The Negro newspapers, largely loyal followers of the Republican party and Booker T. Washington, broke with both to endorse unhesitatingly the soldiers and their defender, Foraker, and to criticize the Administration's handling of the episode. But as the 1908 Republican National Convention approached, most of the newspapers resumed their loyal and submissive pose. The black community, ready for organization, could find no source of leadership here.

The Negro press gave little coverage to the Brownsville affray initially. The press did not make the issue prominent; it utilized the episode when others did. Until Foraker and the Constitution League challenged the assumption of guilt, all of the black papers assumed the soldiers had perpetrated the raid, and many of them justified it. The Staunton (Virginia) *Reporter* asserted a point of view that was common to many of the papers: Such is the kind of justice the Negro always gets; the whole must suffer for the acts of the few. The provocations do not matter; the troops were expected to do nothing to protect their lives. The *Texas Freeman* was more dramatic: "Beating, burning and lynching Negroes by white men it appears is all right with Roosevelt, but the idea of Negroes defending themselves and not kissing the hand that smites them is all wrong." The *Iowa State Bystander* repudiated any who wished to shield the guilty, "but in the name of fairness and common justice give each man a square deal." The *Indianapolis World* also called for the punishment of the guilty men but at the same time lauded the comradely ties which silenced the innocent. This paper repeated the cry of many of the others: "It is the old trouble which causes the Negro to suffer so much in this country — the many must suffer for the sins of the few." The Cleveland *Plain-Dealer,* while asserting that "it's probably true that a handful were guilty, acting under no real provocation, and the rest won't tell," defended the soldiers' right to silence on the grounds that the inspector who interviewed them had no judicial function. The editorial denounced Roosevelt's action as unprecedented and the penalty too severe and imposed without due process of law. The Cleveland paper asked, as did many others, why the officers, who had invariably been held responsible in the past for such exhibitions of lax discipline, had not been held accountable. The *Cleveland Gazette* endorsed this editorial, which it reprinted, taking exception only with the assertion that the men acted without provocation. On the contary, the *Gazette* claimed, the men acted "in defense of their lives." The President's action is an "undeserved and unmerited triumph of southern prejudice." The St. Louis (Missouri) *Globe-Democrat* defended the soldiers by asking: "What about the white offenders who started the disorder?"

Only the *Chicago Public* raised the issue in an anti-military context. The paper denounced Roosevelt's unjust action, but expressed little concern about the results, "because the more the autocratic character of Army life . . . is disclosed . . . the better . . . . These Negroes are to be congratulated upon being put out of the man-killing trade, but President Roosevelt is hardly to be congratulated upon his idea of fair play."

Many newspaper editorials expressed pride in the unwillingness of the soldiers to accept repeated humiliations. The Seattle *Republican* was typical: "Accustomed to clubbing any Negro they had a desire to do the Texas fire-eaters were terrible [*sic*] set back one day last week when a number of Negro soldiers not only refused to be regulated, but actually turned regulator themselves. The soldiers almost razed Brownsville, Texas, to the ground." Lawlessness is not to be encouraged, the newspaper quickly added, but it was desirable to regulate "those devils in Texas."

The *Voice of the Negro* was so anxious to defend the soldiers that it embellished the facts to make the case more convincing. The magazine related various indignities perpetrated upon the soldiers and in doing so confused and distorted them. For instance, the article referred to an incident in which the soldiers, walking along the street, were jostled by a group of white men and women. A white man knocked a soldier down, but later one of the women present claimed she had been assaulted. "A howling mob attempted to storm Fort Brown and met a hail of lead. As a consequence one obstreperous Texas ranger is dead and another wounded. It taught the mob a lesson."[3] The following month the journal repeated the story.

Regardless of the newspaper's previous editorial commitment, all of the black papers defended the soldiers in some way and criticized the severity of the punishment. Even the *Rising Sun*, which rarely criticized the Republican Party in its news stories, had to come to terms with Brownsville. Ordinarily this paper dealt in fiction, gossip, jokes and fashions and gave only limited coverage to those issues which were of such magnitude as not to be ignored. The Atlanta riot, which consumed the black press in general, was given minimal coverage in the *Rising Sun*, and then in such a way as to suggest that the Negroes were somehow responsible. The Brownsville episode was long overlooked by this paper. Editorials dealt with the issue obliquely by ardently defending the Republican party and its contributions to the Negroes of America. By mid-November even the loyal *Rising Sun* was shaken. A very small item on Brownsville included the wail: "No place in this country is the negro safe from the stern severity of the powerful white man."[4] Finally in early December the paper burst out with its one cry of rebellion and then lapsed back forever into loyal silence. It listed all the appointments Roosevelt had made from the black community, but concluded with a reference to the "disgraceful dismissing of the colored troops. . . . The days of the John Browns are over. . . . The leaders of the Negroes must come from within their own ranks."

The *Colored American Magazine* had similar concerns, but from a different vantage point. Loyal not to the Republican party as much as to Booker T. Washington, this magazine ordinarily dealt with matters of poetry, needlework awards, YMCA news and National Negro Business League information and left controversial questions alone. Brownsville was an issue which no black spokesman or voice dared ignore. This moderate journal tried to offend none by praising Foraker for his just and courageous defense of the Brownsville soldiers at the same time it ran a lead article by John C. Dancy, a Roosevelt appointee, who praised the President as a true friend of the Negro.[5] In 1908 the magazine supported Taft on the grounds that the dismissal of the soldiers was solely Roosevelt's responsiblility. As for Roosevelt himself, his effort to reinstate those Negroes who could prove their innocence "ought to be satisfactory, although we notice that some of the less responsible Negroes say that not one should apply unless all are taken back." The Negro, in any case, has no choice. The black voter cannot vote for a party that has the unanimous support of all the Tillmans and Vardamans North and South.[6] The last reference to the Brownsville affray in the *Colored American Magazine* reflected its ambivalence: satisfaction with the testimonials given to Foraker for the "long and bitter fight he waged for justice for the 'Black Battalion' " while expressing great confidence in the "admirable selection of retired army officers chosen to restore the innocent of the discharged Negro soldiers."[7] There is no reference to the outcome of the board's examinations.

The three leading black newspapers, the New York *Age*, the *Washington Bee* and the Indianapolis *Freeman*, whatever the differences among them, and there were many, ultimately evolved to the same position on the Brownsville issue. An examination of that evolution exposes the pitifully dependent position of the Negro press.

The Indianapolis *Freeman* described itself as a "conservative" journal. A strong supporter of Washington, its news and editorial columns regularly lauded Negroes who established successful businesses; stressed thrift and hard work; admonished lazy Negroes to work more diligently; and exhorted the disproportionately large criminal element within the ranks of black Americans to change its ways. Du Bois described this paper as "one of the most important publications among Negroes."[8]

The *Freeman's* endorsement of Washington was ordinarily total if not especially high-level. For example, in its editorial November 1, 1906, the *Freeman* criticized the Cleveland *Journal* for comparing Washington with a certain school teacher in Atlanta. The *Freeman* found the comparison odious because Washington owned a home, was president of a college and had founded a school, and yet was to be compared with a man who "has done nothing but draw salary as an ordinary school teacher."[9]

In the weeks following the Brownsville incident only one brief news story appeared in the *Freeman*, an excerpt from the New York *Evening Mail*. The Negro is a good soldier, the excerpt read, but in peace time "he is inclined to be assertive of his equality." The solution is not to send him to locations where trouble can be expected. Another short news item appeared on November 10, but not until November 24, three and a half months after the incident, was the first editorial published. Unwilling to defend the dismissal of the soldiers and yet reluctant to attack Roosevelt, the editorial placed the blame on the one-sided report of Inspector-General Garlington, a Southerner, who is "in perfect sympathy with the South in its hatred of a Negro behind a gun, or who in any fashion stands shoulder to shoulder with a white man."[10]

By December the Brownsville affray had reached national prominence; during that month it received almost daily coverage in the *Freeman's* news columns and editorials. A lead story reprinted a letter allegedly written by "a soldier's wife," a letter which appeared widely in the black press that month. It began with the assertion that none of the soldiers wanted to go to Texas, having heard of the response of the Brownsville citizens to their impending arrival. Once there, the soldiers were confronted with segregated bars, but they were determined to cause no trouble and so established a place of their own. This alternative did not satisfy the community; quite the contrary, for "Southerners can't stand the spirit of independence in the Negro." The next day a white woman falsely charged a soldier with assault. The letter is careful not to assert the innocence of the soldiers, but rather emphasized that all the soldiers were accounted for at the time of the raid and that the men were not tried by a military court or found guilty of any crime. "Simply to pacify a State where race prejudice reigns supreme no just consideration is given."[11]

The following week's issue again devoted its lead space to the Brownsville episode which it described as "the topic of the hour." Excerpts from leading newspapers were reprinted, news stories of protest meetings were highlighted, but the *Freeman*, still reluctant to attack the President, referred favorably to the "conservative race journals which have been unwilling to believe that the President was properly informed."

To Roosevelt's accusation in his annual message that the black is especially prone to the crime of rape, the only criticism the *Freeman* expressed was that "the President conceded too much to those who habitually place this charge at the door of the Negro." It concluded with the recognition that "the worthy Negro, notwithstanding, will accept the President's well-meaning advice on law and order and decency in the spirit that it is offered."[12]

Later in the month another editorial discussed the President's stubborn personality as a factor hindering a reasonable settlement of the case. The unfortunate truth is, the editor exclaimed, that the ardor with which the Afro-American and his friends have fought aroused the fighting blood of President Roosevelt and "rather than have his enemies boast that they 'brought him to bay,' he will stand by his discharge order to the last ditch."[13] The extensive coverage given the Brownsville case in December fell off abruptly in January and thereafter. In mid-January the *Freeman* still assumed the soldiers to be guilty but was concerned about the many innocent who were punished. In this spirit, the newspaper supported the Foraker resolution to establish a congressional investigation.[14]

No doubt with Booker T. Washington in mind, the *Freeman* dealt with the silence of the "colored office-holder of the higher grades" on the Brownsville question. The radicals have no entanglements with the Republican party, said the newspaper, and so are free to attack the President. The conservatives are dependent upon Roosevelt for their livelihood. While they could not defend the President, the "only dignified and consistent attitude left for them, in this particular instance, was one of silence." Surely this was a defense of Washington, who at this time was still silent on the Brownsville case despite his frequent public addresses.

From this time on, the *Freeman* devoted less and less space to the Brownsville case. At the same time it would not desert the united black community. A June editorial criticized "agitators" but conceded that the soliders had not been proven guilty. The *Freeman* was in an awkward position, and yet managed temporarily to extricate itself by condemning the testimony placed before the President as "trumped-up." In an effort to please everybody, the editorial described Foraker as "honorable and honest as we think the President is honorable and honest." Overlooking its earlier comments on Roosevelt's stubbornness, the editorial concluded with the statement that if the congressional investigation proves the soldiers innocent "we do not think that a man like Roosevelt will feel that he has been put in a hole. His position declares him the very individual to right wrongs."[15]

As the 1908 presidential conventions approached, the *Freeman* occasionally expressed concern over the political ramifications of Brownsville. "The disaffection is widespread and of a nature far different than anything hithertofore dealt with," the paper warned. The major consideration has become a "loss of confidence in the party" which equals a "loss of confidence in the country." Hopefully, Roosevelt will "hit on some happy plan" by which all such confidence can be restored. As if to appease all factions, the *Freeman* continued to admire Foraker: "No other man excepting Charles Sumner. . . has declared so unequivocally for the Negroes."[16]

Brownsville received no further attention for two months and then Foraker was sharply criticized for doing what the *Freeman's* earlier editorial had advised — restoring the confidence of the Republican party by attempting to end the split. In reporting on Foraker's speech which described the President as a "most loyal, patriotic and energetic citizen," the paper analyzed Foraker's conciliatory words thusly: "Senator Foraker befriended the Negroes. . . . He also is a politician. . . . He has made his peace. . . leaving many of the leading Negroes in a very sorry plight. Senator Foraker is in the fold and they are — well, where are they?"[17]

Not for two months more was the Brownsville affair again news; again the dilemma of the *Freeman* was exposed. Congressman Burton was defeated in his race for the mayoralty of Cleveland, and Henry C. Smith, editor of the radical black journal, the *Cleveland Gazette*, was jubilant. In his editorial he credited Burton's defeat to the Negro disaffection over Brownsville. In the final lines of the editorial he threatened that unless justice was meted out to the black battalion, there would be no Republican president the following year. The *Freeman* was indignant at such a threat and urged that the Brownsville affair now be forgotten, "regarding it as some miserable mistake, at least until the truth is known. . . . We contend for continued relation with the party." The *Freeman's* editorial concluded with a statement of support for Foraker's efforts to reunite the party.[18]

The ability of the *Freeman* to continue to straddle was increasingly strained. Although one editorial conceded that the result of the whole episode was "cold comfort to the many innocent soldiers," and that the hearing called for a "very backward procedure, the rule of law being that the individual must be proven guilty," part of the responsibility for the unfortunate situation, the *Freeman* insisted, rested with those who agitated at a time when "hands should have been off." What should be done? "It will be wisdom to allow the whole business to become a closed incident" if the "race is to enjoy continued relations with the party."[19]

Thereafter the Brownsville case received less and less coverage as support for Taft increased. The campaign for Taft began on December 28 with the statement that he had not been very favorably considered by the Afro-American people since "the unfortunate Negro soldiers' happening. . . . of necessity he stood with the President; but he was the victim of circumstances."[20] In the weeks following, Taft's record was examined carefully and found satisfactory. In a January issue a letter from "a prominent colored man" appeared which referred to Taft's New England and Ohio abolition stock; his kind treatment of the Filipinos during his administration there; the promotions granted to colored men in army and civil positions in Cuba. It concluded with the belief that if War Department evidence pointed to the reenlistment of most of the discharged soldiers, surely Taft could be counted upon. The writer in whose column this letter appeared, added: "There is much food for reflection for the colored people in this plain-spoken case. Study it."[21]

Still the Brownsville case would not be quieted. In the midst of the paper's pro-Taft efforts, an editorial dealt with the report issued by the Senatorial investigating committee. The report, the *Freeman* maintained, proved that only a few men were implicated. With a certain wistfulness, it concluded with the hope that the President "may see his way clear to make peace out of the confusion" without involving Congress and thereby a new "threshing out of the 'Negro problem' before the public."[22]

Not long after this plea, a way out seemed to appear in the form of the Administration-backed Warner bill. Although the newspaper had previously criticized the assumption of guilt implied in this bill, it no longer raised that issue. Instead, it claimed that since the guilt of no individual had been established, the logical outcome of the measure would be the reinstatement of practically every soldier who chose to return. "At least it seems that a solution of this vexatious problem has been reached, and the country can now turn its attention to other issues of pith and moment," — presumably the impending presidential election.[23] As a final recognition of political necessity, the *Freeman* supported Foraker's postponement of his bill until after the election in the interest of Republican party unity. After all, the majority of the soldiers "are employed and will suffer no hardships between now and December."[24]

A short while later the *Freeman* spoke its last on Brownsville. It returned again optimistically to the hope for compromise. "The spirit of compromise should come to the relief of the situation." Somewhat surprisingly, the editorial switched to support the Foraker bill, on the grounds that it was better calculated to get the men back in the service. "If the President is inclined to the shortest way out of an ugly muddle, it seems that he would favor the measure with that end in view." The paper did not change its position by withdrawing support from the Warner bill. In its own terms it had been consistent: support that which will end the issue as quickly and as painlessly as possible.

A similar dilemma was expressed in the *Freeman's* most popular column, "Thompson's Weekly Review." Two weeks after the Brownsville raid, Thompson proudly acknowledged the guilt of the soldiers. The real responsibility belonged to the whites whose taunts and jeers made them the aggressors. "Southerners have yet to learn," he went on, "that lynching strange, defenseless blacks in the backwoods is one thing, but firing on the flower of Uncle Sam's army is quite a different thing." He opposed the decision to remove the troops. "If the black boys are to be sent away from every community at the request of some cheap nobodies, they would soon

become like unto the 'Wandering Jew.' " He ended with the proud declaration
that it would be a daring ruffian who would venture to attack these soldiers,
and therefore "it is safe to call the affair a closed one."[25]

Several weeks later Thompson dismissed the rumor that Roosevelt had
threatened to discharge the entire battalion. "Such an order does not sound
like President Roosevelt." If the guilty men cannot be located, the only
course of action is to follow the example of courts-martial when a white
person is accused of a crime — dismiss the case for lack of direct evidence.
Even the guilty men should be dealt with compassionately because of the
mitigating circumstances. And now that the troops are out of the South, such
an incident is not likely to happen again "in a decade"; the best thing to do
would be to let the matter drop.[26]

When the troops were discharged, Thompson was outraged. "Press and
public among the Afro-Americans of the country are stirred to their
depths. . . . Not since the overthrow of the Sumner Civil Rights Law by the
United States Supreme Court, more than twenty years ago, has such a storm
of disapproval emanated from the colored people of the land." Had the
announcement been made earlier, he commented, there would have been a
disastrous slump in the colored Republican vote for Congress in the states
where blacks held the balance of power.

Whatever the intensity of his anger, Thompson maintained faith in
Roosevelt's "sense of fair play and his natural love for the boys in blue." The
columnist was sure that when it could be shown that there was no conspiracy
to shield the criminals Roosevelt would reopen the case. Surely the President
upholds the doctrine that better ninety-nine go free than one innocent man
suffer. At this point Thompson placed the blame upon General Garlington's
biased reporting, and he commended Taft for withholding, however briefly,
the dismissal order. Until a fuller investigation, he said, the Afro-Americans
were willing to suspend their indignant judgment of the President. Thompson
still assumed the soldiers were guilty and still justified them: "the persons
who met death or injury got what might have been expected from the 'rough
house' they wantonly started."[27]

The following spring Thompson still withheld judgment. "I am satisfied
that, at the psychological moment, 'Teddy' Roosevelt will come forward with
a ringing statement on the situation that will electrify the country, and make
every Negro as rampant for Roosevelt as when the gospel of the 'door of
hope' first fell upon the ambient air." His faith withstood time well, for the
following autumn his position was, if anything, more strongly in support of
the President. Relying upon the appeal of secrecy, he referred to the visits to
the President by men of prominence who spoke with a "frankness that can
not yet be made public." There were assurances that the Administration
would not permit the stigma to remain upon a single member of the battalion

longer than was necessary. The President's action was based upon the official report of a trusted subordinate, and the blame should rest with those who misled the President, rather than with the Chief Executive himself. For the first time Thompson doubted the guilt of the soldiers and expressed confidence that "all errors in judgment will be righted, full restitution for losses will be made and the dove of peace will hover smilingly over the race and the administration."[28]

As the months passed and the Senatorial investigation continued, Thompson upheld his faith. In the winter, as rumors of the reports circulated, Thompson maintained that "If any man is found to have been a victim of injustice, it is reasonably certain that President Roosevelt will see to it that proper restitution is made. It will be well for the colored people to restrain their emotions until the case is finally disposed of." In the meantime opinion was that the majority would find the soldiers responsible for the shooting, while the minority would contend that their guilt had not been established by the evidence — exactly what did occur. Thompson added that it was regarded as "highly probable" that if the Senate sustained the minority report, Roosevelt, for the first time since the beginning of the investigation, would be in a position to take definite action. Thompson's optimism, as usual, was misplaced. There never was much chance that the Senate would adopt the minority report, largely because Roosevelt and his supporters opposed it.

When the report finally appeared, Thompson adopted a "plague on both your houses" attitude. Although the report substantiated what Thompson had predicted two weeks before, he repudiated it when it came out because it "indicates a division of sentiment that satisfies nobody, proves nothing, and leaves the whole situation in a condition almost as chaotic as before." Again he disassociated Roosevelt from the affair by claiming that "few level-headed Negroes" believe Roosevelt discharged the soldiers because they were black, but that he was misled by those damaging reports of his trusted subordinates "who had no good blood for the Negro soldiers and who were willing to go to any length to rid the army — or Brownsville at least — of their presence."[29]

However superficially Thompson approached the Brownsville case from the beginning, he concluded with a valid insight.

> In making the soldiers' cause a political issue, with the prestige of the administration swaying in one balance and the personal fortunes of an element of the Republican party in another, with the Democrats "egging on" both sides, with the hope of destroying all concerned and putting the Negro out of the army in toto, the poor black man is being ground to death — and the Republican party is being disrupted.[30]

The *Freeman* was in an embarrassing position. Before Roosevelt's role was clearly defined, it eagerly defended the soldiers, all the while acclaiming

Roosevelt's commitment to a "square deal" for the Negro soldiers. Dissatisfied with the dismissals, the weekly first blamed Roosevelt's subordinates. As the months passed, the only alternative for those who did not wish to encourage disaffection from Republican ranks was silence, broken occasionally by an unspecified plea for conciliation and compromise.

The New York *Age*, among the most influential of the black newspapers, was also one of the most sophisticated. Its approach to the Brownsville case revealed the difficulties facing the Afro-American community in attempting to find and follow a consistent and principled leadership from within its own ranks.

The *Age* was one of the first newspapers to give early and widespread coverage to the Brownsville story, and typically, both assumed the guilt and applauded it. "The infantrymen who fought men's battles on many fields, would not stand for such treatment from cheap civilians and repaid it, to the dismay of the Crackers." The fifteen or so soldiers, according to the *Age* were fired upon by white citizens and defended themselves to such good effect that one white man was killed and another wounded, while no soldier was hurt. Ordinarily throngs of white men would have poured into Brownsville. In this case there were frantic efforts, instead, to remove the soldiers "whose courage might easily become contagious." The government, always compliant to the wishes of the "dear Southerners," ordered the withdrawal of the soldiers "and white Texas has sent up a sigh of relief."[31]

The same issue carried an editorial announcing that it was clear that "the Afro-American and his rights are no longer a part of the policy of the Republican party. . . . the Republican party simply accepts . . . wrongs of the Southern States as fixtures with which the party has no concern at all."[32]

The Brownsville story continued to get wide coverage, with page-one stories almost weekly. The paper continued to claim that "it is highly probable. . .that the soldiers acted on the defensive."[33] The rumor, which proved to be false, that the soldiers were to receive a military trial was applauded by the *Age* editors.[34] By the fall, the *Age* began to question the guilt of any of the soldiers and to defend their right not to become informers. It is the business of the state, the paper said, not the soldiers or even the Federal Government, to discover its own evidence. There is a prevailing notion, the paper went on, that it is the responsibility of the Afro-American to discover his own criminals.[35] It is an outrage, an editorial repeated the following month, to demand that innocent men help the legal authorities "spy out and deliver practically to the mob black men alleged to have committed one sort of crime."[36]

While the *Age* continued to refer to Roosevelt's decision as "executive lynch law" it did not accuse the President of acting from anti-black motives. The only element in the situation which was related to the color question, according to one editorial, was in the provocation by the Texas community.[37]

Suddenly the *Age* began to waver in its position. The newspaper reiterated its position that "the President made a great mistake," but expressed concern that the agitation and condemnation "will be overdone." Surely appeal, in the proper time, to the public, to Congress, to the courts, would set things right.[38] Yet when the preliminary report of the Constitution League was issued the newspaper temporarily returned to its earlier more militant stand. "If Mr. Roosevelt, with his impulsiveness as a man and President, ever went off half-cocked before," wrote Archibald Grimké in his column, "he certainly went off half-cocked in the Brownsville affair." Using a recurrent image, the President was again accused of lynching these men by executive decree in much the same way as the mob lynches its victims on mere suspicion.[39]

For the first time the *Age* questioned automatic endorsement of the Republican Party. Negroes have "instinctively" voted Republican because they felt the treachery in the Democratic Party, on the one hand, and because they have never responded to third parties, on the other. "But William McKinley and Theodore Roosevelt, as the vile R. B. Hayes before them, have done much to shake their faith in the wisdom of sticking to the Republican party in the future."[40]

The *Age* also examined the Brownsville case in terms of political deals. It suggested, for example, a possible arrangement in the case of Senator Blackburn of Kentucky, who gave Roosevelt invaluable support during the Brownsville debate, and had since been given a "very juicy plum" on the Isthmanian Canal Commission. Similarly, Senator Edward H. Carmack of Tennessee, always a bitter opponent of Roosevelt's, supported him on the Brownsville case, and in return had a friend appointed to the visiting board for West Point.[41] While these two men may have been rewarded for their staunch support of Roosevelt on this issue, it is hard to imagine that their positions would have been otherwise.

In the spring the *Age* ran appeals for funds to defend the soldiers and described the Constitution League as working "by means of organized lawful resistance and positive action, to aid in suppressing lawlessness, mob violence, lynchings, and all forms of the murder spirit."[42] In the same edition, though, appeared a surprisingly moderate editorial. It began with kind words for the President's genuine compassion for the Afro-American. Certainly, it continued, Roosevelt did not realize what a furor his order would create, but when the explosion came he stood by his order because he thought he had the right. "He thinks as much of the Afro-American people now as ever he did. But having got the bit in his teeth he will keep it there. He is built that way." The editorial concluded ambiguously by "regretting" the Brownsville order from many points of view. The political situation created by it, or made possible by it, prejudiced the interests of the Republican Party at large and the interests of the Afro-American people in all their relations as citizens.[43]

But as late as September the *Age* remained highly critical of Roosevelt and the Republican Party and continued to refer to the possibility of supporting a Democratic presidential candidate. "In Afro-American newspapers and conventions and private conversation, antagonism to President Roosevelt because of his Brownsville order . . . has become so pronounced as to compel all men to sit up and make note. The great and good things the President has done are submerged by the howling sense of personal injury." In another editorial in the same issue: "By making the Brownsville order and the Southern policy of the Administration his own, Secretary Taft wrote Ichabod all over the face of his candidacy. This cropping out in every direction." And later: "Afro-American politicians who are staggering in the dark will do well to keep their eyes on Charles Evans Hughes . . . because it is written in the stars that he will be the next President."[44]

So read the *Age* in September. By October, after Booker T. Washington purchased the newspaper, the position was reversed. The widely reprinted editorial entitled "The Brownsville Ghouls" expressed the change in policy. The next week the *Age* announced that "the anti-administration movement is being inspired, guided and financed by certain white men for their own selfish purposes . . . many of the colored men who are so unselfishly devoting their time and talents to this agitation are men without any specific employment or visible means of support."[45] Thereafter, the Brownsville hearings, which had been given extensive coverage, were almost ignored. Simultaneously came increased and favorable coverage of Roosevelt and Taft.

As the criticisms from the more militant black papers mounted, the *Age* was forced to the defensive. To the repeated charges that the *Age* was controlled by Washington, the editorial answered: "It is not true. . . that Dr. Booker T. Washington owns *The New York Age*, or any part of it. He does not own it and he does not control it."[46]

To the complaints directed at the *Age's* changed position on Brownsville, the newspaper had this to say: "The *Age* has expressed itself on the President and his dismissal. . . . we felt he had made a mistake and inflicted a grave wrong on our race. . . . We do not believe in continually keeping the same subject before our readers and perhaps if the editor of the Philadelphia *Pilot* would learn the same lesson his paper would have a larger circulation." This statement of November 28, 1907[47] was the last word to appear on the Brownsville controversy for three months. The long silence was broken by a reprint from an editorial in the *Independent*, somewhat gratuitously described as "always a tried and true friend of the Negro people" which urged Negroes not to disavow Taft, for if he is not the best he is better than the

Southern Democrats.[48]

When the Senatorial investigation was completed and the reports were issued, the press, black and white, gave wide coverage to it. Except the New York *Age*. A small story in the middle of the second page announced the issuance of the three reports. No editorial appeared.[49] The following week a full-page story on Taft had the headline: "Secretary of War Taft Pleads for the Negro . . . Says Electoral Qualifications Should Apply to White as well as Colored Men."[50]

The *Washington Bee*, ultimately to make the biggest reversal of all the Negro papers, was one of the first to attack Roosevelt. Less than two weeks after the Brownsville incident, the *Bee* spoke editorially with pride of the soldiers' aggressiveness. "Colored soldiers are not cowards."[51] In a news story, indistinguishable from the editorial, appeared the statement that "Any other government but the United States would have turned those colored soldiers loose and permitted them to protect themselves. . . . The entire State of Texas with several surrounding States included, could not have defeated those colored troops." Roosevelt was the villain and Foraker the hero. But if Foraker was to be the hero, he must be unblemished. Thus, the paper defended the Senator's position on the railroad rate bill, claiming that the "colored man was the bone of contention" even in this issue.[52]

Two open letters in the editorial column addressed to George B. Cortelyou, chairman of the National Republican Committee, challenged the President's right to dismiss the soldiers, accused him of adopting southern mob tactics, denounced him for not daring to act before the election, and threatened him with Negro disaffection from the party.[53]

The *Bee* expressed the notion, as did many other newspapers, that any soldier turned over to a civil court, as a result of having been exposed by a comrade, would be endangered. The *Bee* admitted the possibility that some of the enlisted men and officers knew who the "real perpetrators of the crime were" but would not deliver up one of their comrades "to be burnt alive by scoundrels." Had any soldiers been given to the Brownsville civil authorities, surely "there would have been a lynching bee the next night."[54]

Although the *Bee* did not share Washington's point of view in general, and not at all in the Brownsville case, it was unwilling to attack him for his silence. "A few prejudiced individuals" hold Washington responsible for the "childish order" of Roosevelt's.[55]

The *Bee's* criticism of Roosevelt was severe. "The attacks of Tillman, Vardaman and others have not done the race half the harm that Mr. Roosevelt has since he has been President." And again the question, asked by this and many other papers: "Why didn't he discharge the commissioned officers as well?"[56]

Another open letter to Cortelyou the following month reflected the desperate quality of the newspaper. "I notice that the Department of Commerce and Labor is appointing quite a number of Jews now. . . . The Jews are on top under this administration and the colored man is at the bottom. . . . The Democrats, Jews and Catholics are getting all they want."[57]

The *Washington Bee* warned: "Mr. Taft may be nominated for President, but there is one thing certain, and that is the colored voter of the country will not support him."[58] Instead, "the country is with Senator Foraker."[59]

The *Bee* made slight overtures to the Democrats, claiming that the two Democratic administrations of Cleveland protected black employees, and that it was only men like Tillman and Vardaman who prevented the Democratic Party from functioning honorably.[60]

As the Senatorial investigations continued, the *Bee* was convinced that the "Texas crackers" shot up the town and not any of the soldiers. Senator Foraker is weaving a web around the neck of President Roosevelt "so perceptible that a mule can see it as he runs."[61] In early March the newspaper was still anti-Roosevelt. In an open letter to the President the paper declared that "the colored Americans have fared worse under your administration than they have under any administration since the founding of the government."[62]

Before the month was over, the *Bee* was falling into line, with as much grace as the situation permitted. Calling upon the memory of Charles Sumner, who ultimately submitted to his party, "we must bow to the will of the great majority. . . . If the Republican party says Taft, and if the Negroes of this country prefer the Republican party to the party of Tillman, Vardaman, et al, there is nothing left for us to do but to join. . . . The *Bee* recognizes that the party is greater than any man, and that the tail cannot wag the dog."[63] Within a few weeks came an attack on Trotter and the "so-called Negro Conferences which call for support of Vardaman, Tillman and others."[64]

In the next several weeks, news coverage of the Brownsville investigation diminished sharply, while the ground was being prepared for support of Taft. An anonymous "prominent colored representative" was quoted on April 25 as follows: "An impression, studiously created in the East, that Secretary Taft is opposed to the interests of the colored people. . . and that the colored people . . . are opposed to him has been largely dispelled."[65]

With the Republican convention only weeks away, the *Bee's* editor, Calvin Chase, who had previously expressed the opposite sentiments, challenged the "few disgruntled and disappointed colored Republican politicians" who asked the colored voter not to support Taft if he is nominated.[66]

By September the *Bee* had become as vitriolic and as ardent a supporter of its new position as it had been of the earlier one. The paper claimed that the Brownsville agitation had never been undertaken sincerely but had always been used to embarrass the Administration. The *Bee* now had information that certain Negroes had been hired to agitate the Brownsville matter and "to inflame the passions of unthinking and unreasonable Negroes to a white heat — even to the point of anarchistic utterances. Now who paid these Negroes?" The *Bee* admitted that it had described as "impolitic" an editorial in the New York *Age* which classified these Negroes as Human Ghouls who were not searching justice but thirty pieces of silver. But, the *Bee* went on, it was not then in possession of certain information that certain Negroes were under pay to agitate the Brownsville matter "simply as a dirty political means to a contemptible end with the race as the loser."[67]

Finally, the *Bee* unskeptically accepted the confession of discharged soldier Boyd Conyers as proof of the guilt of the soldiers.[68] Finding the guilty men "will wipe out the stain of disgrace from the innocent men" while it "makes a fool of so many of our race who have been denouncing the President so bitterly. A valuable lesson has been learned: it never pays to resort to unreasonable criticism of men and officials until we have all the facts."

The final story on Brownsville ended with praise for the President who more than any other "has seen so little of the Irish, the German, the Welsh and the Negro in a man, and more the real worth, honesty and nobleness . . . and that is why the great body of the well thinking members of the race refused to attribute his discharge of the colored soldiers to their color."[69]

The *Bee's* new position did not go unnoticed or uncriticized. The *Baptist Truth* wrote of the *Bee's* having "fallen from grace." As for the *Bee* now stating that Foraker's chances for the nomination are nil, that was always so, as the *Bee* should have known. "We ought to be men or we ought to go back in slavery," said the *Baptist Truth* and added that until Roosevelt and the Republican Party correct the brutal treatment of the Negro soldiers there is no office or political job in Washington to buy its favor.[70]

Although most of the black press ultimately supported Roosevelt and Taft, a few newspapers did not. The *Broad Ax* consistently publicized the Brownsville story in its pages and finally endorsed Bryan in 1908. While some newspapers may have held, and some even voiced, criticism of Booker T. Washington, few were willing to attack him so sharply and so relentlessly. Washington, the paper declared, who "has proven himself to be the cringing slave of Roosevelt and Taft, desires the ten million Negroes in this country fall down and worship him as their infallible god!"[71]

When a news release asserted that Washington had met with Taft and assured him that he had the support of the Negro people, the *Broad Ax* described Washington as "getting himself ready to pull his fat leg for more money, so that he could be in a better position to fling it out to the hungry Colored newspaper men, which will enable them to tout him as being the greatest white man's 'Nigger' in the world."[72]

The news columns referred regularly to the growing disaffection of the Afro-American community with the Republican Party. In 1904, said the *Broad Ax*, a Negro seconded the Republican nomination for President and a black and white child, waving American flags, walked down the aisle and stood on the platform together. At the 1908 convention, however, the Negro was kept in the background. A few resolutions were included but "as a sop to the Negro." The Republican attitude toward the Negro is better illustrated by the replacement of Negro delegates from the Southern states with lily-whites who were chosen to occupy their seats.[73] If Roosevelt or Taft had little to offer the black voter, what did the *Broad Ax* suggest was the advantage of supporting Bryan? First, William Jennings Bryan is a good man, the indication seeming to be that Mrs. Bryan was extremely cordial to the *Broad Ax* representatives at the Democratic convention. Second, it is tactically wise for the Negro to vote Democratic, so as to be able to exert pressure on both parties. And finally, taking off from Du Bois' dictum to vote for an avowed enemy rather than a false friend, the *Broad Ax* declared that an administration directed by Vardaman would be better for the Negro than one headed by Taft because there would be no pretensions to friendship.

In their campaign to win their black readers to Bryan, the editors occasionally resorted to something less then sensible, though not necessarily ineffective, arguments. One sensational story had the headline: "Taft Headquarters Has Jim Crow Elevator. Administration Race Press Is Mighty Quiet About This Insult in a Northern City."[74]

An anonymous letter was reprinted with the opening, "I am not a Negro . . . but were I . . . I would vote against Taft." The author dealt largely with Roosevelt's handling of Brownsville, referred to Taft as "Roosevelt's shadow" and concluded by claiming that Cleveland, who received no Negro votes, treated them better than had Roosevelt, who got them all.[75]

During the period when there was growing belief in large black disaffection from the Republican Party, the *Broad Ax* gloated, prematurely as the election returns indicated. President Roosevelt is just beginning to realize, said a news story, that

> Booker "Taft" Washington, Ralph W. Tyler, William T. Vernon, Charles W. Anderson and a few loud-mouthed Negroes here in Chicago who are ever ready to turn traitor to their race and sell it out for a little money or a few cheap jobs, are unable to whip all the Negroes into line for Taft, as they had promised to do, and are taking alarm over the revolt of the Negroes against his "man Friday" for President, and the part he played in the Brownsville affair, in order to smooth out matters with the Negro who has for many years been the blind political asset of the Republican party.[76]

Foraker was initially viewed by the newspaper as "the greatest of all the champions of human rights."[77] When he proved anxious to return to the Republican good graces he was described as a "tricky politician." "Senator Foraker has turned summersault, filled up on black crow and has come out in favor of Taft."[78] But when the election was long over, the editors returned to their original evaluation and wrote of Foraker as one "who will go down in history as one of the greatest statesmen that this nation has ever produced, and after more than two years of hard fighting. . . finally triumphed. . . thus finishing his imperishable work. . . in a blaze of everlasting glory."[79]

The *Horizon, A Journal of the Color Line*, published in Chicago by W.E.B. Du Bois, F.H.M. Murray and L.M. Hershaw had a short life but an impressive one. Its position on Brownsville was consistent and sober. The *Horizon*, alone among black publications, recognized that the President's decision, while it was probably influenced by his insensitivity to the Negro, was based upon broader considerations. The magazine challenged Roosevelt on two grounds: that he might discharge an enlisted man from the army over the man's protest in the absence of a court-martial's findings; and, granting the power, that the evidence on which the order was based was sufficient and conclusive.

The *Horizon* was also able to recognize that not all enemies of its enemies are friends, that is, that some of the opposition to Roosevelt on the Brownsville case was rooted in opposition to Roosevelt and had little to do with justice. The editors divided the press as follows: the organs of the former slaveholding power unanimously endorsed the President's order; the organs of the North which accept the doctrine of administration infallibility, endorsed; the independent organs, condemned; and the organs of monopolies and trusts, perhaps seeking an opportunity for revenge, condemned.[80] Hershaw later referred to the "strange and almost unaccountable circumstance" of the "ardent friendship suddenly displayed for the race" by some newspapers heretofore indifferent or hostile to measures to secure justice for Negroes. "This is particularly true of the New York Sun which used to exclaim in and out of season, 'No force bill; no Negro domination.' Does the Sun really shine for all?"

Referring to the Brownsville affair as the "American Dreyfus case," the *Horizon* expressed the hope that there would soon be proof as to who did the shooting. Nevertheless, "the fact remains that these men, suspected and unsuspected alike, and all, were hustled out of the army under a cloud of disgrace, without an opportunity to establish their innocence or even to answer their accusers." The magazine did not assume the soldiers to be guilty, even initially, and then defend them, nor did it later assume them to be innocent. The editors did not even accuse Roosevelt of a deliberately anti-Negro act or of being duped by prejudiced subordinates. "We do not accuse the President nor any of his subordinates of any intentional injustice," Murray carefully said. "But since some of our race, who are individually helpless and un-equipped for the task, are the immediate sufferers – we must not flinch, but properly and persistently press our views on the President and his advisers until his convictions yield."[81]

An unsigned appeal, with the ring of Du Bois' style, urged the President to reconsider his act.

> This is the chance of your career. You have done wrong . . . . So have others . . . . You have acted hastily, impulsively and doggedly. So all men act who think strongly and feel deeply. . . . I will not say that the 25th Infantry have absolutely proven their entire innocence, but I do say. . . that they have raised doubt as to their guilt. . . . You have con-victed them. You thought them guilty. . . . Their guilt is today un-proven. You know it is unproven. . . . The nation is watching you. The black millions are waiting. Theodore Roosevelt, are you an honest man? If so, speak.[82]

Roosevelt did not act as he did out of anti-black feeling, the *Horizon* asserted. "I do not really think," said an unsigned editorial, "he ever knew a colored man intimately as a friend." His contacts with the Negro community were limited to politicians or "men who have humored his whims. Consequently, he feels in no way drawn to the black population . . . as he is, for instance, toward the South. . . . Without doubt he thought he was doing justice. The trouble is, and the crime lay, in the impulsive, unthinking judgment. Yet in this respect he is not different from his fellow. He is an American. The pity of it is, we expected more."[83]

NOTES

1. From the *Freeman*, February 9, 1907.
2. "The In-Look," *Horizon*, January, 1907.
3. October, 1906, "Our Monthly Review" section.
4. November 15, 1906, p. 1.
5. April, 1909.
6. May, 1908, editorial.
7. April, 1909, editorial.
8. Du Bois to Gardner Richardson, March 10, 1910.
9. Page 4.
10. November 24, 1906, p. 4.
11. December 6, 1906, page 4.
12. December 15, 1906, p. 4.
13. December 29, 1906, p. 4.
14. January 19, 1907, p. 4.

15. June 22, 1907, p. 4.
16. July 27, 1907, p. 4.
17. September 28, 1907, p. 7.
18. November 30, 1907, p. 3.
19. December 7, 1907, p. 4.
20. Page 4.
21. January 11, 1908, p. 1.
22. March 14, 1908, p. 4.
23. March 28, 1908, p. 1.
24. May 23, 1908, p. 1.
25. September 1, 1906, p. 1.
26. October 27, 1906, p. 1.
27. November 24, 1906, p. 1.
28. October 12, 1907, p. 1.
29. March 7, 1908, p. 1.
30. *Ibid.*
31. August 23, 1906, p. 1.
32. Page 4.
33. August 30, 1906, p. 6.
34. September 6, 1906, p. 1.
35. October 25, 1906, p. 4.
36. November 8, 1906, p. 4.
37. November 29, 1906, p. 4.
38. December 13, 1906, p. 4.
39. December 27, 1906, p. 1.
40. February 23, 1907, p. 4.
41. March 7, 1907, p. 2.
42. April 4, 1907, p. 1.
43. April 4, 1907, p. 4.
44. September 5, 1907, p. 4.
45. October 24, 1907, p. 4.
46. November 21, 1907, p. 4.
47. Page 4.
48. February 27, 1908, p. 4.
49. March 12, 1908, p. 2.
50. March 19, 1908, p. 1.
51. August 25, 1906, p. 4.
52. September 1, 1906, p. 4.
53. October 27, 1906, p. 1; November 10, 1906, p. 1.
54. November 10, 1906, p. 4.
55. November 24, 1906, p. 4.
56. *Ibid.*
57. December 8, 1906, p. 1.
58. December 21, 1906, p. 4.
59. December 29, 1906, p. 1.
60. January 26, 1907, p. 4.
61. February 16, 1907, p. 4.
62. March 2, 1907, p. 1.
63. March 28, 1908, p. 4.
64. April 11, 1908, p. 1.

65. April 25, 1908, p. 1.
66. May 9, 1908, p. 4.
67. September 26, 1908, p. 4.
68. *Infra.*
69. December 19, 1908, p. 4.
70. Quoted in the *Washington Bee*, April 18, 1908, p. 1.
71. May 2, 1908, p. 1.
72. July 4, 1908, p. 3.
73. June 20, 1908, p. 1.
74. August 1, 1908, p. 1.
75. October 3, 1908, p. 2., signed with initials J.T.C.
76. August 15, 1908, p. 1.
77. April 18, 1908, p. 1.
78. September 5, 1908, p. 1.
79. March 6, 1909, p. 1.
80. January, 1907, Vol. I, No. 1, no page.
81. February, 1907, pp. 19–20.
82. March 7, 1907, pp. 7–8.
83. January, 1907, Vol. I, No. 1, no page.

PART III

THE NATIONAL POLITICAL SCENE

VIII

THE PRESIDENTIAL RESPONSE:

ROOSEVELT AND TAFT

Theodore Roosevelt

O President! O can it be!
That within yourself you feel
You are giving to the innocent
What you have termed "square deal"?
Men are included in your writ
Whose terms were nearly through,
Their country served with honor, sir,
Think, what would Jesus do?

In spreading justice out so broad
With "muck rake" trying to teach
Don't blot a good man's entire life
Because he failed to peach.[1]

Although Theodore Roosevelt's policy toward black Americans may appear to be inconsistent, one can make sense of it by recognizing that it was rooted in the racist assumptions prevalent in the United States, but tempered, when necessary, by the demands of politics, and when possible, by a genuine

133

humanitarian impulse. Roosevelt frequently had good instincts concerning the Negro people in the United States, but these spontaneous feelings were not part of a serious or thoughtful commitment to a concept of equality, and so it was not difficult for him to repudiate them when the political pressure mounted.

In contrast to Woodrow Wilson, for example, Roosevelt was incensed by the "appalling brutality" of the East St. Louis riot in 1917. In a Carnegie Hall speech honoring Russia, he said: "I am not willing that a meeting called to commemorate the birth of democracy in Russia shall even seem to have expressed or have accepted apologies for the brutal infamies imposed on colored people . . . . Let there be the fullest investigation into these murders." Roosevelt's remarks were a response to Samuel Gompers' claim that racial violence had occurred in East St. Louis because employers imported Negroes.[2]

Roosevelt was not an unprincipled man. Where he had strong feelings, he remained consistent. In the area of rights for black Americans his feelings vacillated and therefore so did his policies.

The famous Booker T. Washington dinner was the first incident that involved Roosevelt, the President, in the Negro question. In October, 1901, Roosevelt invited Washington to the White House for a conference and to dinner. The details regarding that occasion have been clouded, somewhat deliberately, by Roosevelt and his supporters. Washington was neither invited to a luncheon nor to dinner spontaneously, as was later claimed, for in the Roosevelt papers there is a note, dated October 16, 1901.

Dear Mr. President: I shall be very glad to accept your invitation for dinner this evening at 7:00.[3]

"The reaction to Booker Washington's dinner at the White House in the first month of Roosevelt's presidency was startling in its violence, even in a day of high-pitched racial propaganda," C. Vann Woodward has observed.[4] The New Orleans *Times-Democrat* in a comment typical of many others, asserted that "when Mr. Roosevelt sits down to dinner with a Negro, he declares that the Negro is the social equal of the white man." The incident was described by another newspaper as "the most damnable outrage ever."[5] Although Roosevelt stated that he would invite Washington to dinner as often as he wished, Washington never again ate in the White House.

Roosevelt made many important changes in the policy of the Republican party in the South, and while his policy changes sometimes received the support and at other times the condemnation of the black community, it has been demonstrated that Roosevelt's personal attitudes toward Afro-Americans played a small part in his decisions.[6] Roosevelt announced that he would not "appoint an improper man to a ; osition because he is a Negro, or with a view of affecting the Negro vote; or on the other hand . . . exclude a proper man from an office. . .because he is a Negro." "Essentially he observed this tenet," remarked John Morton Blum, for "he discriminated not on the basis of color but on the basis of [Mark] Hanna."[7] The one unwavering principle of his use of patronage in the South "was his surer control of the Republican party."[8] Roosevelt was concerned lest the cohesive organization Mark Hanna had developed during the McKinley Administration would challenge Roosevelt's hold over his party.

To aid him in strengthening his position in the Southern Republican machine, Roosevelt used the talents and knowledge of Henry Clay Payne of Wisconsin and James C. Clarkson of Iowa. He also used Booker T. Washington. In relation to the Booker T. Washington dinner, "the clamor of Southern whites over the racial implications of this dinner obscured the immediate significance of the occasion. Washington's mission was political."[9]

In the early stages of his southern policy, Roosevelt carried out several changes that infuriated the white South and endeared him to the black community. For example in the fall of 1902 Roosevelt repudiated the anti-black activities of the southern lily-white machines in several southern states. "Then early in January, 1903, he closed the post office at Indianola, Mississippi, because of white demonstrations against the Negro postmistress."[10]

The outburst from the white South was astonishing; Roosevelt was perplexed. What he had not realized was that "his first administration happened to coincide with the climax of Southern racism. . .and although his challenges to Southern mores were fewer, they were more spectacular and considerably more widely publicized than those of any recent President."[11] Roosevelt began to reexamine his policies. With "the Hanna threat dispelled, and the election of 1904 handsomely won, he returned to the task of winning the South."[12] After a successful trip through the South, "little more was heard against Roosevelt's racial views."[13]

The reaction of Afro-Americans was predictably one of profound disappointment. The *Voice of the Negro* surveyed fifty black leaders for their opinion of Roosevelt's course; only ten approved.[14] The revised southern policy, which was later to be embraced wholeheartedly by Taft, was well established when the Brownsville incident took place.

Roosevelt's three major addresses devoted to the Brownsville issue, and the variation from one to the other, reflect the defensive quality of his position and the hurtful blows he must have felt were struck by Foraker, the Constitution League and other critics.

The President ordered the Secretary of War on November 5, 1906, to comply with the recommendation of General Garlington. On November 9, Secretary of War Taft issued an order, by the direction of the President, that the members of Companies B, C and D, Twenty-fifth Infantry, certain members of which organizations "participated in the riotous disturbance" which occurred in Brownsville, Texas, on the night of August 13, 1906, "will be discharged without honor from the Army by their respective commanding officers and forever debarred from reenlisting in the Army or Navy of the United States, as well as employment in any civil capacity under the Government."

When Congress convened in December 1906, Foraker offered a resolution calling for an investigation and this brought, on December 19, a bristling message from the President. It was based on the investigation by the Inspector-General's staff, but it was far more positive and authoritative concerning the guilt of the men than were the official reports.[15]

Roosevelt began by expressing his satisfaction at being able to present to the Senate the facts "as to the murderous conduct of certain members . . . and to the conspiracy by which many of the other members . . . saved the criminals from justice, to the disgrace of the United States uniform."

His evidence was based on the reports of Major August P. Blocksom; of Lieutenant-Colonel Leonard A. Lovering; and of Inspector-General Ernest A. Garlington. That Garlington is a Southerner is irrelevant, Roosevelt said; Lovering is from New Hampshire and Blocksom from Ohio. But the fact of birthplace of any officer is one which "I absolutely refuse to consider."[16] Precisely the same action would have been taken, Roosevelt went on, had the troops been white—"indeed the discharge would probably have been made in more summary fashion." Blocksom's report was based upon the testimony of "scores of eyewitnesses" and it "established the essential fact beyond chance of successful contradiction."

In tracing the history of the difficulties between the citizens and the troops of the garrison, Roosevelt, admitting that there was a conflict of evidence as to the responsible parties, concluded that "there was blame attached to both sides."

The following facts "in my judgment can not be successfully controverted": from nine to fifteen of the black soldiers took part; they shot at whomever they saw moving; in some of the houses were women and children "as the would-be murderers must have known."

The soldiers were the aggressors from start to finish. "The act was one of horrible atrocity, and, so far as I am aware, unparalleled for infamy in the annals of the United States Army."

The effort to refute this narrative by suggesting that the townspeople shot one another to discredit the soldiers is "an absurdity too gross to need discussion and unsupported by a shred of evidence."

There is no question, the President went on, that many of the comrades of the murderers privy to the deed have combined to shelter the criminals and these men have rendered it necessary either to leave all the men, including the murderers, in the Army, or to turn them all out. Under the circumstances there was no alternative, for the value of the Army would be at an end if such an outrage were permitted.

The evidence "proves conclusively" that a number of soldiers engaged in a cold-blooded and cowardly act, the purpose being to terrorize the community, and at a time when resistance was out of the question and identification of the criminals impossible. "A blacker crime never stained the annals of our Army." Every effort was made to persuade those innocent of murder to separate themselves from the guilty by helping bring the criminals to justice.

This discharge from service was not a punishment, Roosevelt explained. It was not punishment, for punishment for mutineers and murderers is death. "I wish that it were possible for me to have punished the guilty men." These men were under contracts of enlistment and it was the President's clear duty to terminate those contracts when the public interest required it. "It would have been a betrayal of the public interest on my part not to terminate the contracts which were keeping in the service of the United States a body of mutineers and murderers."

"Any assertion that these men were dealt with harshly because they were colored is utterly without foundation," Roosevelt asserted.

Roosevelt then volunteered several precedents. Many took place during the Civil War when companies were disbanded for "mutinous behavior." In one case in 1862 members of a regiment had stolen goods from a store. When the guilty men were not discovered, General Grant mustered out the two officers and fined the regiments. While one might reasonably claim that such a precedent weakened rather than strengthened Roosevelt's case, he chose to see that "in its essence this action is precisely similar to that I have taken, although the offense was of course trivial."

Members of one regiment in 1860 lynched a barkeeper who had killed a soldier. Unable to discover the culprits, Colonel Robert E. Lee disbanded the company, transferred the men to other companies and discharged them at the end of their enlistment without honor. In 1864 Lee disbanded a regiment for cowardly conduct, stating that he regretted that some of the innocent men were forced to share the common disgrace.

Roosevelt concluded his address by admonishing the blacks in the country not to defend their guilty members, for it might mean damage to the white race but it would mean ruin to the black race.

Foraker, in the Senate on December 20, effectively challenged much of this message. Roosevelt probably recognized that the evidence was insufficient and his authorative manner overstated, for he sent Assistant Attorney-General Purdy to Brownsville for futher investigation, and on January 14, 1907, he transmitted another message.

Roosevelt's second message was more precise and restrained.[17] Instead of a number up to twenty implicated in the raid, it was "some person or persons." Roosevelt then offered in detail the evidence of shells, cartridges, bandoleer, as well as the eyewitness reports, so that "the fact that the assailants were United States soldiers . . . would be conclusive . . . . if not one soldier had been seen . . . and if nothing were known save the finding of the shells, clips, and bullets." The "scores" of eyewitnesses translated into fourteen.

The additional evidence taken, he declared, corroborated his earlier order. However, that section that barred the men from all future civil employment was found to be "lacking in validity" and so was revoked. The dismissal shall remain in force, he insisted. But if any one of the men discharged is able to prove himself clear of guilt, or of shielding the guilty, he will be reinstated.

If in essence the order was upheld, the tone was different.

Foraker continued to collect evidence for the defense throughout 1907 and he presented it to the Senatorial committee. Did Roosevelt feel he had made a mistake? During 1908 he spent $15,000 in Government funds for private detectives to seek additional evidence.

On December 14, 1908, Roosevelt sent another message, a far less categorical message, to Congress, describing the result of the latest investigation.[18] The investigation, he said, fixed "with tolerable definiteness" some of the criminals "who took the lead in the murderous shooting of private citizens at Brownsville."

It established clearly, he went on, the fact that the soldiers did the shooting. The investigation had not gone far enough to enable him to determine all the facts, but it had gone far enough to determine with suffcent accuracy certain facts of enough importance to make it advisable that the report be placed before the Senate. It appears that almost all of the members of Company B must have been actively concerned in the shooting, either to the extent of being participants or to the extent of virtually encouraging those who were. As to Companies C and D, there can be no question that practically every man in them must have had knowledge that shooting was done by some of the soldiers of B troop, and possibly by one or two others in one of the other troops. This concealment was a grave offense, and it was aggravated by their testifying before the Senate committee that they were ignorant of what they must have known. It can be said in partial extenuation that they were probably cowed by threats made by the more desperate of the men who had actually been engaged in the shooting as to what would happen to any man who failed to protect the wrongdoers. Moreover, there are circumstances tending to show that these misguided men were encouraged by outsiders to persist in their course of concealment and denial. "I believe we can afford to reinstate," the President continued, "any of these men who now truthfully tell what has happened, give all the aid they can to fix the responsibility upon those who are really guilty, and show that they themselves had no guilty knowledge beforehand and were in no way implicated in the affair, save by having knowledge of it afterwards and failing and refusing to divulge it."

"I recommend that a law be passed," he went on, "allowing the Secretary of War, within a fixed period of time, say a year, to reinstate any of these soldiers whom he, after careful examination, finds to have been innocent and whom he finds to have done all in his power to help bring the guilty to justice." Meanwhile the investigation would be continued. The results made it obvious that only by carrying on the investigation as the War Department had carried it on was there the slightest chance of bringing the offenders to justice, or of separating, not the innocent, for there were doubtless hardly any innocent, but the less guilty from those whose guilt was heinous, the President concluded.

The tone of the last message was sober and straightforward, with renewed assurance that his order had been indeed the correct one but without any of the bombastic quality that dominated his earlier public statements.

When Roosevelt reopened the case in 1908 he found Foraker more bitter than he had ever been. Roosevelt had by then exposed Foraker's connection with Standard Oil. His presidential aspirations had been smashed.

On January 12, 1909, Foraker rose to say his last on Brownsville. According to Roosevelt, former Private Boyd Conyers of B Company had admitted the leadership in the riot. Foraker then read an affidavit from Conyers denying the entire story. Within a few weeks Roosevelt went out of office. The whole Brownsville matter is omitted by Roosevelt from his *Autobiography,* perhaps an indication of his real attitude toward it.

* * * * *

As did many in his time, Theodore Roosevelt believed in the superiority of the Anglo-Saxon race. In a letter to his close friend, Owen Wister, he described Booker T. Washington as one of the "occasionally good, well-educated, intelligent and honest colored men," but in general "as a race and in the mass they are altogether inferior to whites."[19]

Roosevelt's beliefs included nonwhite people abroad. At one point, concerned over the actions of Latin American nations, he declared his intention to "show those Dagos they will have to behave decently."[20]

"Make it as strong as you can to Beaupré," he ordered on July 14, 1903. "Those contemptible little creatures in Bogota" ought to understand how much they are jeopardizing things and imperiling their own future. Later he added that "we may have to give a lesson to those jack rabbits."[21]

Roosevelt was also a well-bred upper-class gentleman – a product of American Victorianism. Great changes in society, culminating in extraordinary material progress, created in large sections of the upper and middle classes a mood of comfortable smugness and complacency which later generations have found among the most unattractive of Victorian characteristics. Roosevelt embodied most of its worst qualities: the smugness, the self-righteousness, the parochialism, the superficiality, the priggishness.

Roosevelt chose not to identify with the other side of Victorianism, with those who were its most active and corrosive critics or with those who brought into this period a breath of humanity and a sensitive honesty of spirit. It becomes less easy to excuse or explain the Theodore Roosevelts when we realize that he was born in the same generation as Thorstein Veblen (born one year before Roosevelt); John Dewey (born one year after); or William James (born in the previous decade); when we realize that John Stuart Mill's essay on "Liberty" and Charles Darwin's *Origin of the Species* were published when Roosevelt was a year old, and Karl Marx's *Capital* within ten years after that.

Roosevelt was narrow-minded and self-righteous. As a legislator his attitude toward labor legislation indicates that he was "both ignorant and prejudiced."[22] During the Haymarket case, Roosevelt had written that he would have shot down the rioters. When the case was on appeal he said that all Americans would benefit if the "Chicago dynamiters" were hanged.[23]

When he decided to do something it not only became right for him but right for everyone because it was then possessed of virtue and morality. "I am the father of three boys [and] if I thought one of them would weigh a possible broken bone against the glory of being chosen to play on Harvard's football team I would disinherit him."[24]

Roosevelt would no more read Rabelais, he told his son, than "examine a gold chain encrusted in the filth of a pigpen."[25]

In 1915, under oath, he testified as follows:

Q. How did you know that substantial justice was done?
Mr. Roosevelt: Because I did it, because I was doing my best.
Q. You mean to say that when you do a thing thereby substantial justice is done?
Mr. R.: I do. When I do a thing I do it so as to do substantial justice. I mean just that.[26]

He had, despite an occasional insight and wide knowledge, a "tissue of philistine conventionalities, the intellectual fiber of a muscular and combative Polonius."[27] He had, too, a preference for the heroic virtues of the fighter, not the virtues of one engaged in the struggles of his day, but those qualities associated with the fantasy life of one who finds repulsive both the problems of the masses and the materialism of the rich: the cowboy, the frontiersman, the soldier, the hunter.[28]

Because of his commitment to authority and discipline, he was undoubtedly outraged by what he was sure the soldiers had done. However much he may have been forced to soften his tone in his public addresses, his letters indicate his mounting fury, stubbornness and sense of persistent righteousness. As late as 1908 Roosevelt was still capable of strong feeling, as expressed in a letter to Herbert Parsons:

> Tell the negro or white agitator who declaims about Brownsville that he is standing up for murder and occupies a position in its essentials like that occupied by the defenders of the bomb-throwers in Chicago or New York or Patterson, and hound him out of companionship with decent men.[29]

Confronted with a challenge to his authority and a serious breach of discipline, Roosevelt's response to the Brownsville episode was, if not inevitable, certainly not surprising. In a telegram to the Governor of Massachusetts two months after the Brownsville raid, Roosevelt made clear his commitment to Army discipline:

> I feel the most profound indifference to any possible attack which can be made on me in this matter. When the discipline and honor of the American army are at stake I shall never under any circumstances consider the political bearing of upholding that discipline and that honor, and no graver misfortune could happen to that American army than failure to punish in the most signal way such conduct as that which I have punished in the manner of which you complain. There has been the fullest and most exhaustive investigation of the case.[30]

Roosevelt was indeed a racist, but he was probably right when he claimed that his actions would have been the same had the soldiers been white. There was little room for the weak and helpless, white or black, in his outlook which glorified the valiant and strong man. While he did not callously pursue a policy that was purposefully unjust or based upon anti-black premises, his limited compassion and his inflexibility prevented him from perceiving with any profundity or reasoning with any depth or feeling with any genuine connection to his fellow man, regardless of race, creed or color.

William Howard Taft

William Howard Taft inherited the unpleasant Brownsville episode and its aftermath. As Roosevelt's Secretary of War he had executed the discharge order, and subsequently Taft said: "I am not responsible for the Brownsville order; but I think it entirely justified."[31]

Yet Taft's role in this affair suggests a more moderate and thoughtful approach. In late 1906, for example, he believed that it would be better, as he suggested to the President, to have a rehearing "as it always is where a decision is questioned." If a rehearing shows that the original conclusion was wrong, it presents "a dignified way of recalling"; and if it does not, it enforces the original conclusion.[32]

Taft was not in Washington when Roosevelt ordered the discharge of the soldiers. He was not familiar with the case, but in view of the number of protests he found awaiting him when he returned to Washington, he telegraphed the President who was then himself out of the capital, suggesting that the dismissals be halted pending further inquiries into the guilt of the soldiers. Taft was particularly impressed with the request from Mrs. Mary Church Terrell, and it was largely on her urging, as well as Booker T. Washington's, that he withheld the execution order and telegraphed to Roosevelt recommending a rehearing.[33]

But "the silence of the President," Taft explained, "and futher disclosure . . . that [he] had refused to suspend the order on the application of a number of gentlemen, made me feel that I was doing something which was altogether a violation of my duty, so I withdrew my direction . . . . I had hardly done this before I received word from the President that he had given the application for a rehearing full consideration and could not grant it unless they satisfied him by additional evidence."[34]

Considering the different personalities of the two men, it required considerable concern for Taft to have done what he did. He continued to maintain a level of sobriety and care in the investigation, however little influence he may have had. It was he, for example, who pointed out to Roosevelt the conflicting testimony of Paulino Preciado, who claimed to have been an eyewitness to the murder of the barkeeper. Taft, in studying the earlier Grand Jury evidence, discovered that Preciado's testimony immediately after the episode was significantly different. Taft sent the information to Roosevelt and asked that it be forwarded to the Senate with his message and other papers.[35]

When Taft read Gilchrist Stewart's accusation that the townspeople were responsible for the attack, he did not, as Roosevelt did, automatically dismiss the charge as absurd, but wrote to the President asking "Is this within the limits of possibility?"[36]

Years later Taft, in a letter to Henry Cabot Lodge, complained of how Foraker had pounced upon the Government's use of private detectives. Taft's letters indicate that he, at least, in good faith had endorsed the use of detectives in the hope that they would establish the guilt of the specific soldiers. Nothing short of determining individual guilt appeared to be satisfactory to him. While he defended the use of Government-hired detectives, Taft admitted that "had the course been taken earlier, before the order, I believe it would have developed all the facts."[37]

As late as 1912 Taft had not lost interest in the incident. He requested that Secretary of the Interior, Walter L. Fisher, make Mingo Sanders eligible for appointment as a "messenger without respect to the civil service rules." It was clearly established that he was innocent of the shooting. His offense, if any, was that he failed to disclose the names of the guilty parties. For this offense, under the conditions that existed then and the inadequate discipline that the officers were shown to have exercised, "I feel that he has been severely punished. He has suffered more than any of his companions who were discharged because he was so near retirement."[38]

Taft was not an especially imaginative or aggressive man. He maintained Roosevelt's southern policy. His attitude toward the problems blacks faced in America was not better, perhaps a bit worse, than Roosevelt's. But he was a man with a steady and understated sense of integrity. Had Roosevelt permitted him to supervise the entire episode, undoubtedly the Brownsville affair would have been more satisfactorily handled.

NOTES

1. From the *Washington Bee*, January 26, 1907.
2. Elliott M. Rudwick, *Race Riot at East St. Louis, July 2, 1917* (Carbondale, Ill.: Southern Illinois University Press, 1964), p. 134.
3. Quoted in Henry F. Pringle, *Theodore Roosevelt, a Biography* (New York: Harcourt, Brace and Company, 1931), p. 175.
4. C. Vann Woodward, *Origins of the New South*, p. 464.
5. Quoted in Pringle, *Theodore Roosevelt*, p. 175.
6. In addition to the above sources, see Henry F. Pringle, "Theodore Roosevelt and the South," *Virginia Quarterly Review*, IX (1933), 14-25; and Seth M. Scheiner, "President Theodore Roosevelt and the Negro, 1901-1908," *The Journal of Negro History*, XLVII (July 2, 1962), 169-182.
7. Blum, John Morton, *The Republican Roosevelt* (New York: Athenium, 1962), p. 46.
8. *Ibid.*, p. 47.
9. *Ibid.*, p. 44.
10. Woodward, *Origins of the New South*, p. 464. General examination of Roosevelt's policies in the following pages.
11. *Ibid.*, p. 465.
12. *Ibid.*
13. *Ibid.*, p. 466.
14. "A Canvass for Opinion," *Voice of the Negro*, II (1905), as quoted in Woodward, *Origins of the New South*, p. 466.
15. "Special Message, the Senate," *Messages and Papers of the Presidents*, XVI, 7320-37.
16. *Ibid.*, 7329.
17. *Ibid.*, 7737-41.
18. *Ibid.*, 7347-48.
19. July 27, 1906, *Letters of Theodore Roosevelt*, V, 227.
20. Quoted in Ray Ginger, *The Age of Excess, The United States from 1877 to 1914* (New York: The Macmillan Company, 1965), p. 61.

21. Quoted in Pringle, *Theodore Roosevelt,* pp. 218-19.
22. *Ibid.,* p. 55.
23. Ginger, *Age of Excess,* p. 61.
24. Pringle, *Theodore Roosevelt,* p. 332.
25. *Ibid.,* p. 333.
26. *Ibid.,* p. 314.
27. Richard Hofstadter, *The American Political Tradition and the Men Who Made It* (New York: Vintage Books, 1956), p. 229.
28. See Hofstadter's discussion of Theodore Roosevelt, *American Political Tradition,* ch. IX, 206-237.
29. April 10, 1908, *Letters of Theodore Roosevelt,* XVI, 4675.
30. To Curtis Guild, Jr., November 7, 1906, William H. Taft papers, Library of Congress.
31. Taft to C. P. Taft, January 1, 1907, Taft papers.
32. *Ibid.*
33. Letter to Senator Charles Curtis, Topeka, Kansas, July 14, 1908, Taft papers.
34. *Ibid.*
35. January 14, 1907, Taft papers.
36. Undated communication, 1906 folder, Taft papers.
37. January 18, 1909, Taft papers.
38. August 5, 1912, Taft papers.

IX

JOSEPH B. FORAKER

We hail thee, noble chieftain from the West!
  Lo! twenty years we've seen thee dare to be
A knight! Where some stooped ignominiously
For gain or power, still thy soul's high quest
Was honor for the land thine honor blessed,
  And justice for her sons of every degree
  Branding great wrongs, and false "diplomacy,"
Crusader,thou hast served thy country best!
  The race must die that hath no noble men! —
  Ideals, not idols, make a people great.
"Do justice, tho' the heavens falls!" — Again
  The Roman call that roused the listless state
Thou sound'st; and, crying — "SHAME TO GIVE MEN LESS!"
HAST PUT THY RACE ON TRIAL BY NOBLENESS![1]

Theodore Roosevelt was out to get Foraker, and he did. Although the two men had frequently been political allies there had long been many and serious differences between them. Foraker, very much the conservative, had a "genuine conviction of the righteousness of big business."[2] They battled over Roosevelt's reform measures. Foraker, for example, vigorously opposed the President on the Hepburn bill. They also battled over foreign affairs, Foraker believing that Roosevelt encroached upon the Senate's power. Foraker opposed Roosevelt's intervention in Cuba in September 1906 on the grounds that the Platt amendment gave Congress, not the President, the power to intervene. But it was Foraker's split with Roosevelt on the Brownsville affair that so angered the President that he determined to eliminate Foraker from political life.

It is not difficult to understand why this issue, among all the other more serious and far-reaching ones, should have enraged Roosevelt. The other differences between the two were essentially differences of principle, differences in attitudes toward business and government. They were real differences, and each advocate could confidently and securely feel that his position was correct. The battle was a legitimate battle between two politicians. But on Brownsville, Roosevelt erred badly. His initial impetuousness was compounded when he refused to withdraw gracefully. Instead, he persisted in his decision and thus exposed himself more and more. He ultimately demanded support not on the basis of justice but of party loyalty. Foraker attacked with enormous skill. He made Roosevelt appear the fool, and he the wise one, Roosevelt the unjust and he the just, Roosevelt the racial bigot and he the patriot. All Roosevelt could do in response was sputter and bluster, and then he took revenge.

Roosevelt could write to Brooks Adams that the community did not support his position on Brownsville "and I didn't very much care."[3] But surely he did care, for if a reformer is to dedicate his political energies to the community, is it not important that the community understand and be grateful? Did Roosevelt believe what he said to Adams: "I believe you are right in saying that Foraker has been representing Wall Street in attacking me on this issue"? Such an accusation was a favorite one of Roosevelt's. He repeated it two years later. "The entire agitation over Brownsville was in large part," he said in a published statement in 1908, "not a genuine agitation on behalf of the colored men at all, but ... the effort by the representatives of certain law defying corporations to bring discredit upon the administration because it was seeking to cut out the evils connected with ... the corrupt alliance between certain business men of large fortunes and certain politicians of great influence."[4] The theme reappeared in letters to his friends. "The real and underlying reason for attacking me about the Brownsville incident has nothing to do with the negro, but represents simply the purpose of the great capitalistic reactionaries to do damage to the policies for which I stand."[5]

Even if there were merit to such a charge, the specific accusations remain. Foraker's motivation is one thing, the questions he raised quite another.

Roosevelt's unrelenting anger at Foraker was noticeable by the unorthodox manner in which he displayed it. In addition to the conventional methods — eliminating him from patronage decisions and isolating him politically – he attacked him publicly and inappropriately at the Gridiron Club in a somewhat shocking display of bad manners.

Champ Clark described the Gridiron Club as the most famous club in America. Its membership, limited to forty, was composed entirely of Washington newspapermen. It had a long waiting list as well as a small number of honorary members. The invitations were sent out without solicitation. They could not be bought. The club had two rules: first, "Ladies are always present" – which they never were; second, "Reporters are never present" – and they always were, in large numbers. The first rule was a warning to all speakers that they use only "chaste language." The second rule meant that guests could speak freely without fear of being reported.

> I saw and heard a debate [said Clark in January 1907] before two or three hundred men between President Roosevelt and Senator Joseph Benson Foraker of Ohio. According to my judgment – to use pugilistic parlance – the bout ended in a draw, although the sympathy of the majority of the audience was with the Senator because he was attacked by the President and was therefore fighting on the defensive. . . . That debate was the culmination of the feud betwixt him and the President, which practically eliminated him as a presidential candidate.[6]

Here was the setting: a table on a raised platform ran the whole length of the big dining room in the New Willard Hotel. Those who were to speak and other very prominent people were sitting at the table. The other tables ran into the speakers' table at right angles, making the famous Gridiron. In time Roosevelt was called on for a speech. He spoke for about thirty minutes with the utmost vigor about railroad-rate regulation and reform legislation in general. Then he opened up on the Brownsville quarrel, justified his actions and stated that he would brook no interference from anybody. The situation was very tense. "To put it mildly – very mildly – excitement ran mountain-high."[7] As soon as Roosevelt sat down the president of the club introduced Foraker. When he arose his face was as white as a sheet. In five minutes his "face was as red as the stripes on the flag."[8] While Foraker was speaking Roosevelt was gritting his teeth, clenching his fist, shaking his head and muttering: "That is not so; I am going to answer that; that is not true; I will not stand for it," and similar remarks. Three or four times he started to get up to interrupt Senator Foraker, but was restrained by Mr. Justice Harlan and others.

When Foraker sat down the President jumped up and began his reply. It was red-hot. He said something like this, according to Clark.

> Some of those men were bloody butchers; they ought to be hung. . . . It is my business and the business of nobody else. It is not the business of Congress. It is not the business of the House. It is not the business of the Senate. All the talk on that subject is academic. If they pass a resolution

to reinstate these men, I will veto it; if they pass it over my veto, I will pay no attention to it. I welcome impeachment.

It is not overstating the case, Clark concluded, to say that he took the breath of that audience away — "they fairly gasped."[9]

The story did leak to the press. The *Washington Post* said that it was too important a matter to be hushed up by any rule of the club's etiquette.[10] The stories in the press were substantially the same as Clark's.

Mrs. Julia Foraker reported on the changes Brownsville brought into her life. Invitations to White House dinners ceased. In the early years of Roosevelt's presidency they were repeatedly asked; after Brownsville, never. For almost three years, she wrote, "we were to live in an atmosphere of spying and furtiveness that was like something out of revolutionary Russia."[11]

Subtly a peculiar change came over the atmosphere of her house, she reported. People began to change their calling hours from daytime to evening. Sometimes men sent their wives. "I would receive them and give to my husband the information they brought for us. Then we began to get it — we were being watched."[12] Secret Service men were watching our house, she claimed. "Senator Foraker's mail was tampered with. Spies struck at our social life." Very much in evidence at afternoon receptions, at all functions that could be crashed, was a "gentlemen detective." Everybody knew what he was doing — eavesdropping. As time went on everybody on the inside of things adopted the "hush" note. One talked guardedly, looking over one's shoulder. "We lived for months under this strain."[13]

Mrs. Foraker also reported on an offer to her husband from Roosevelt by way of Senator Penrose. If Foraker would drop the Brownsville fight, Penrose is supposed to have said, Roosevelt was prepared to offer him any distinguished post he might desire. An ambassadorship, perhaps? "This was quite comic, this idea of transporting or rather deporting the troubling Foraker to foreign shores."[14]

When the deplorable mockery was over, wrote Foraker's wife, Roosevelt had won. Something else came out of Brownsville and that was "Roosevelt's determination that Senator Foraker, too potent, too plaguey, too unwieldable, should be banished from political life."[15]

An accurate description, or the exaggerated memories of a loyal wife?[16] If some of the details are fanciful, the outlines are not. Roosevelt was determined to eliminate Foraker, and it was Foraker's opposition on Brownsville that caused the President's determination. Just after Taft assumed the presidency, Roosevelt wrote to him concerning a reluctant candidate in a particular election in Ohio. Roosevelt asserted that the individual's preferences were not paramount; they are "of secondary importance to defeating Foraker."[17] "I regard it as outrageous, from your standpoint and from the public standpoint alike, to consider any personal question whatever as of weight compared with the one vital question of putting in for Senator any decent man who could be elected as against Foraker," Roosevelt went on. "I do not presume," he insisted, "to say what particular step should be taken in order to accomplish this purpose, but . . . I. . . emphatically feel that it was the one purpose which should be held chiefly in mind by all concerned."[18]

Foraker concurred with Champ Clark that the Brownsville affray put him out of the 1908 race for the presidency, but he disagreed with Clark that it also put him out of the Senate, except indirectly, as it aroused Roosevelt's fury. It destroyed whatever chance he might have had for the presidential nomination "not because my course with respect to it was either wrong or unpopular, for the exact opposite was true, but because it made President Roosevelt, then at the height of his popularity and power, openly and actively hostile." Roosevelt was strong enough to nominate Taft, but he was not strong enough "to defeat me" for reelection to the Senate, said Foraker.[19] The Senate defeat, Foraker said, came with a speech made by "Mr. William R. Hearst, at Columbus, Ohio, on the evening of September 17, 1908, in which to make it appear that I had some kind of improper relations with the Standard Oil Company, he read a number of stolen letters to me from Mr. John D. Archibald of that company, showing payments to me at different times of various sums of money."[20] Neither in 1908 or later could Foraker convincingly demonstrate that those payments constituted anything but "improper relations." In 1908 Roosevelt seized on the letters which Hearst continued to publish to force Foraker out of public life.

If Brownsville did begin the end for Foraker, and if Foraker was a politically astute and sophisticated man, what accounted for his unrelenting attack upon the Administration? In a letter to Trotter he stated that he was not a candidate for any office and did not expect to be.

> What I have been doing in the Brownsville matter has been solely be-
> cause of a sense of duty towards an unfortunate battalion of gallant, but
> helpless soldiers. It has been a long hard labor, on account of which I
> have been compelled to tax not only my strength, but my pocketbook
> as well. I have not desired, and do not desire any reward for it, except
> only the consciousness I shall always have that I succeeded in securing
> for them a chance to be heard in their own behalf.[21]

Foraker's financial efforts in behalf of the case appear to have been considerable. When he suggested that Marshall go to Georgia to follow up the alleged Conyers confession, he wrote: ". . . if the Constitution League will not take care of it let me know and I will try to meet it, although I can ill afford to do so at this time."[22] Earlier when efforts were made to reimburse him for his expenditures, he wrote, and this letter as the one above, is typical of many others: "It is generous and thoughtful on your part to make the suggestion. . . but I hope you will not pursue the matter further. I will try to carry the load until we get through with the case and truth is established and justice administered."[23]

Throughout his writings, published and unpublished, Foraker maintained that his commitment to Brownsville was one solely of principle. An early letter to Charles Emory Smith set the tone and established two of the major motivations he consistently maintained. First, "I do not know what the facts may be but I think these men should be given a day in court," and second, "All this aside from the fact that I think it perfectly clear that the President had no constitutional or statutory power to convict and punish these men by executive order." As his investigation continued, Foraker added a third consideration: his belief in the innocence of the soldiers.

How did Foraker explain his involvement in the case? Initially, he said many times, he assumed the soldiers were guilty, that given what must have been great provocations by prejudiced southerners, the soldiers made an effort to avenge the wrongs. But the drastic punishment and the wholesale nature of it caused him to read with some care the testimony on which the President acted. When he analyzed the testimony he saw at once that it was "flimsy, unreliable, insufficient and untruthful," and that, combined with the further fact, as announced in the newspapers, that every man in the battalion under oath denied any guilt, caused him to doubt their guilt and "to conclude that it was my duty, if no one else would do so, to cause an investigation with a view to establishing whether or not any of the men did participate, and if any were found to be guilty, those punished and the innocent acquitted."[24]

When Congress reconvened in December, Foraker offered a resolution directing the Secretary of War to send to the Senate all information on the subject. Debate followed. Foraker charged that while the President has the right to grant discharges in general he does not have the right when it rests upon a conviction of a felony punishable with imprisonment and when, as a result of such discharge, punishment is inflicted as if it had been a result of a court-martial. Where men are charged with the commission of a criminal act they are entitled to a trial before they are condemned, and they have that right even if they are in the Army, Foraker declared. The resolution was adopted and a few days later, on December 19, 1906, Roosevelt sent a message to the Senate. His indignation and irritation were already apparent. Foraker answered the following day, challenging the President's claim that he had the constitutional authority to take the action. Roosevelt had claimed that the discharges were not punishment, for discharge was certainly inadequate to the crime of murder. Foraker answered that punishment need not be adequate to be punishment, that if the men had committed murder it was inadequate and that if they had not, the discharge was harsh and brutal.

Foraker then attacked the political background of Major Blocksom, though from Ohio, the son of a Vallandigham-type of Democrat. Foraker also challenged Blocksom's concluding sentence: "It must be confessed the colored soldier is more aggressive than he used to be," as irrelevant to the case but indicative of his prejudice. At this point Foraker offered in detail, as he was to do again and again, the sequence of events after the firing, concluding, as he did in the minority report, that it was impossible for the soldiers to have participated in the assault.

Foraker also returned many times to the conclusion that whatever Garlington and Blocksom said happened, neither they nor any of the other investigators ever found any evidence whatsoever incriminating any individual.

On the question of precedents, to which Roosevelt had referred, Foraker quoted the Military Secretary in a letter to the secretary of the President that a "protracted examination of the official records has thus far resulted in a failure to discover a precedent in the Regular Army for the discharge of those members of three companies of the Twenty-fifth Infantry."[25] Foraker then effectively challenged the claimed relevance of Roosevelt's flimsy precedents.

In response to Foraker's speech, Roosevelt sent Major Blocksom and Assistant Attorney-General Purdy to Brownsville to secure additional testimony, after which there came another presidential message. This brought on a running debate that continued until January 22nd, when Foraker's resolution authorizing a Senatorial investigation was adopted. He claimed that the men had been condemned without a hearing and that this was contrary to the spirit of American institutions, that it was the duty of Congress to undo that wrong by giving them a chance to face their accusers. At the same time, Foraker said, he hoped that if the investigation established the truth the "President would in a manly fashion undo the wrong he had done."[26]

"I knew he [Roosevelt] was somewhat provoked, but did not realize that his unfriendly feeling was serious, or that he would manifest publicly his displeasure." The Gridiron episode, which took place a few days later, made it clear to Foraker how angry the President was. Foraker in his memoirs reprinted a lengthy letter written to his son at the time of the Gridiron confrontation describing the scene. The picture Champ Clark had drawn of an angry and white-faced Senator vitriolically responding to the battle is not sustained by Foraker's memory, his version being considerably more complimentary to himself. "I was most reluctant to respond. My first thought was to refuse to do so, for I did not feel equal to the occasion, but there then came calls for me from all over the room. I saw that I could not do otherwise, and, therefore, took the floor."[27] Foraker discussed the rumor circulating that his purpose in carrying out the investigation was "that of a demagogue to secure the negro vote."[28] Again he stated that he was after no votes, white or black, but was simply seeking an opportunity for the soldiers to be heard in their own defense and to have justice done.

With feigned modesty, Foraker wrote to his son that he had intended to go up and speak to the President but there was such a rush toward him for some twenty or thirty minutes that he did not notice the President and his party leave the room, "but I am told they went out rather promptly, and without being detained as I was."[29]

Relations between Foraker and Roosevelt, strained before the Gridiron dinner, were nonexistent thereafter. Shortly after, Roosevelt ignored again a patronage recommendation; Foraker made no further ones.

The investigation called for by Foraker's resolution began a few days after the Gridiron Club dinner, and with some interruptions, continued during the sessions of Congress for more than a year, until March 1908, when a majority of the committee reported. Foraker took the floor on April 14, 1908, for one of his most famous speeches, in which he summarized the minority report he and Senator Bulkeley had submitted. Most of his long speech was a summary of the investigation and his analysis of it as it appeared in the minority report. He reiterated his claim that the Senate investigation was to give the men an opportunity to answer the charges that had been made against them. A highly irregular practice, it was a violation of the practice that had been observed since the beginning of the common law for the protection of those who were charged with crime. "Notwithstanding this disadvantage, and the many other disadvantages to which these men were subjected," there was no doubt as to their innocence, he said.

After reviewing the eyewitness testimony, he concluded that there was "not a particle of testimony from any so-called eyewitness that is not either contradicted by the witness himself or by some other witness or which is not shown by uncontradicted testimony as to the effect of darkness on the vision not to have been unreliable if not impossible."[30]

Foraker then discussed the two bills on the floor of the Senate, one introducted by Senator Warner of Missouri and one by himself. Warner's bill provided that the soldiers should be allowed to reenlist upon presentation of proof of innocence satisfactory to the President. Foraker's bill provided that they should be reenlisted on formal application, supported by an affidavit of innocence on all charges. Foraker sharply attacked the Warner bill for its alleged violation of the spirit of our institutions: first, because it required men accused of a crime to prove their innocence; and second, that they must prove their innocence to the satisfaction of a judge who had repeatedly prejudged their case.

The investigation carried out by the detectives, which was financed from the President's contingent fund, only opened up new problems, despite Roosevelt's ringing words to the contrary in his special message to the Senate on December 14.

Roosevelt's message, largely based upon Herbert Browne's report, brought with it renewed attack by Foraker. He introduced a resolution directing the Secretary of War to divulge complete details of the employment of Browne and Baldwin. "His motion was agreed to the following day despite vigorous protest from Henry Cabot Lodge. The Massachusetts Senator objected to this example of the 'usurping of executive function.'"[31]

The Secretary of War's report was submitted to the Senate January 12, 1909. "Embittered by his approaching retirement from the Senate, Foraker attacked Roosevelt and Taft."[32] He began by reciting the history of the several investigations, reports and messages, and explaining how each time the President had pronounced the testimony against the men "conclusive," and how, nevertheless, he had immediately after his answer to each such message sought to get new or additional testimony, which indicated that, notwithstanding his positive assertions, he still had doubt.

He then offered letters he had received and affidavits and official records of the War Department to show that after, according to the President, it had been "thoroughly established" that the men were guilty, as much as $15,000 had been paid to detectives from a balance of what he claimed was a lapsed appropriation, to try to get some real proof, and that "in this behalf every rule of evidence applicable had been violated," and all without securing one iota of proof that he, Foraker, "was not able to refute and destroy absolutely, and did destroy the moment it was offered."

On the appropriation, Taft had information about the source of money which apparently Foraker never discovered. Taft wrote to Brigadier General George B. Davis that there was a law "which I didn't know of, forbidding the use of detective agencies by any Department of the government." Taft recalled that Davis had certified that the contract with Browne was legal and on this basis Taft assured the President accordingly. If it was illegal, Taft went on, he didn't understand why the comptroller had not forbidden it when the money was withdrawn. "He must have those things at his fingers' ends. I presume," he concluded, "Senator Foraker will make the employment of these detectives an occasion for attack and diatribe, and I could wish that he did not have so strong a case in reference to the doubtful character of the authority exercised." Happily for Taft, Foraker overlooked this aspect.

Foraker in his criticism claimed that the President "has resorted to a method in his effort . . . that can not be fittingly characterized without the use of language which, if employed, might appear to be disrespectful to the Chief Executive. . . . It does not lessen the gravity of his offense that it appears to be imperceptible to him or, if not so, that he has become utterly oblivious to all the restraints of law, decency and propriety in his mad pursuit of these helpless victims of his ill-considered action."

Foraker went on to claim that "fraudulent impersonation, misrepresentation, lying, deceit, treachery, immoral use of liquor, coupled with the promises of immunity and the excitement of hope and fear, and the offer of employment and remunerative wages, had been resorted to in order to secure the sought-for testimony." The so-called confessions were not confined to "such actions as might incriminate the parties making them," or to those affected by them, who might be present when they were made, but extended also "to those not present when they were made and who were without any opportunity whatever" to be heard in their own defense.

He cited numerous authorities to show that confessions are never heard as evidence except where shown to be purely voluntary and free from inducement by promise of protection or reward and free from threats and duress. Then Foraker offered the explosive affidavits from Boyd Conyers and others repudiating Browne's report.

Foraker concluded his powerful attack by stating that "as atrocious and indefensible as is the crime of murder, more atrocious and indefensible is a cold, scheming, calculating plot and conspiracy to fasten the crime of murder upon an innocent man."

Foraker's speech exposing the detectives was the last extended one he delivered in the Senate. It proved sufficient, he claimed, for on February 23, 1909, a few days before his term of office expired, he succeeded in getting "a vote on my bill, in an amended form." He had earlier introduced a bill creating a Board of Inquiry to investigate the Brownsville matter. The amendment to it was of such a nature as to alter the bill profoundly. That it was passed by a straight party vote, 56 Republicans for it, 26 Democrats against, the remainder absent or paired, might make one wonder how the bill was turned into a party measure by one who was on the outside.

The original bill provided that five military officers named by Foraker constitute a Court of Military Inquiry. This body would review the Brownsville affray and certify those individuals eligible for reenlistment. Once certified, the ex-soldier was to be reenlisted without presidential approval. Presidential pressure ultimately forced Foraker to agree that the Secretary of War should appoint a Court of Inquiry, to be composed of five officers of the United States Army, not below the rank of colonel, to hear testimony on the case and within one year to report on those qualified for reenlistment. Thus amended, the bill was passed by the Senate on February 2, 1908; four days later the House followed. Roosevelt signed it on March 3 as one of his last official acts.

"I would not have been content with the bill as it passed," wrote Foraker, "had it not been that I knew that with my retirement from the Senate no one would remain in either that body or in the House of Representatives who would champion the cause in which I had so long labored."[33]

The significance of the intra-party controversy surrounding Brownsville was so well known that Champ Clark discussed it openly on the House floor.

There has never been any partisan politics in this thing. There has been a great deal of factional Republican politics in it, as much as there was of partisan politics in the Homestead strike. This Brownsville wrangle removed Senator Joseph Benson Foraker absolutely as a candidate for the Presidential nomination. It contributed largely to an event that I am glad of, and that was the election of the Honorable Theodore E. Burton to the Senate of the United States by putting Senator Foraker out of the running.[34]

Foraker's acceptance of the compromise measure to his bill caused great consternation among his followers, as the voluminous mail questioning him on the subject attests. So considerable was the negative response that Foraker published a reply in a four-page leaflet entitled "Foraker Bill for Restoration of Discharged Soldiers: An Issue in Approaching Campaign: Letter of Senator Joseph B. Foraker to Mr. John B. Milholland Concerning the Postponement of Vote on Brownsville Matter."

The statement is a reprint of a letter to Milholland dated May 22, 1908. Foraker claimed that active presidential opposition made passage of the bill in its original form impossible and passage of any bill before the election impossible. At most he had assurances of only 35 votes, and some of those were wavering. He needed 47. Postponement until after the election was better because, in the first place, "it could not have been worse" than defeat, and, in the second place, it kept the subject alive during the campaign.

He went on to say that the bill was to be passed in December because enough Republicans had promised him their vote if he were willing to wait. With the bill postponed, the issue was living, Foraker insisted, and the ten million colored people had a right to demand of Republican candidates for office, including the presidential candidate, that they pledge themselves to support the Foraker bill as it originally stood.

Such a move did not occur and largely because Foraker, whose leadership would have been essential, did not provide it.

In a letter to Milholland, Foraker scoffed at the idea, rumored in newspapers, that there is "some kind of political make-up being connected with the matter." At the same time Foraker admitted that the Democrats were anxious to drive him to a vote because they knew he could muster only 37 votes at most, and that under the circumstances he did well "to succeed in uniting the Republican party, or practically so, on the proposition to make the bill the special order for December 16."[35] As it turned out, postponing the issue united the party and removed the issue from the campaign. That this was part of Foraker's intention, that he was attempting to make peace, is impossible to determine. Milholland considered the possibility. He confided

to his diary that he had "Recd letter from Sn. Foraker explaining postponement of Brownsville or trying to explain it. Decided by Mrs. F not to publish
it. He will write another year he made a mistake. Chandler says he made a
deal. Crane, Aldrich & Co. put on pressure."[36]

Some months later a memorandum was sent to Roosevelt concerning
peace overtures from Foraker. The correspondent, unnamed in the memorandum, stated that:

> After listening to the Senator's description of the situation in Ohio and
> the possibility that he would be reelected, he read the answer he had
> prepared and published to the Hearst charges. . . . Then he turned to
> Brownsville. "I do not understand why the President has been so antag-
> onistic to me," he stated. "For years we were the closest friends, and
> then my opposition he construed into criticism. . . . In all my speeches,
> I have never said one word against him personally. . . . Do you think
> there is any way a conference could be arranged with the President when
> we could talk over the Brownsville matter? I don't want to fight any-
> body. I am a man of peace." I told Senator Foraker I would see what I
> could do.[37]

No answer to the memorandum was found. Apparently Roosevelt was decided that no rapprochement was beneficial to him. Foraker's vitriolic
criticism of Roosevelt on the Senate floor was made the following month.

When the bill was finally passed some months later, Foraker admitted, it
was not "exactly what I should have had, but the law I did get concedes all
the essential propositions for which I contended."[38] Even that bill, he
claimed, was passed largely because of the successful repudiation of the detectives' evidence. In other words, the easy passage which he claimed was promised during the previous session did not materialize, either because the
Senators changed their minds or because the original promises were never
made.

Roosevelt's response to the amended bill, according to Senator Aldrich
who told Judge West who told Foraker, indicated that ultimately he was
satisfied. Aldrich said he told Roosevelt that some kind of bill would have to
be passed, that the overthrow of the detectives' evidence made further successful opposition impossible, and that when the President finally agreed to
the bill in the form in which it was passed, he remarked petulantly, "That
means every one of them will get back." Aldrich then answered that unless
somebody could come forward with charges, that ought to be the result, to
which the President replied, "I suppose so," and with that dismissed the
subject; but that afterward he seemed to be rather good-natured about it
all.[39] And well Roosevelt should have been good-natured. He had defeated
Foraker for the Presidency, for reelection to the Senate and on the Brownsville issue.

However sincere Foraker may have been, however genuine his compassion for the mistreated soldiers, there is no doubt that he also utilized the episode for political advantage. His papers are heavy with correspondence that makes such a claim irrefutable. At the time he was denying any truth to the charge of presidential aspiration, he was organizing with black leaders to establish Foraker-for-President clubs. As early as January, 1907, shortly after the agitation on Brownsville began, Foraker was in correspondence with J. D. Houston of Georgetown, Ohio, who had established such a club. Foraker even approved, with mild changes, a letterhead that read as follows:

Famous	**O**rator	**R**ouses	**A**ll	**K**inds	**E**nterprising	**R**epublic
Farmers	**O**pulence	**R**esult	**A**fter	**K**eeping	**E**verything	**R**unning
	Opportunities	**R**eward	**A**ll	**K**een	**E**nergetic	**R**eason

Houston wished him a Happy New Year "and the republican nomination for president of the U.S." He liked the letterhead because "something novel like this attracts attention and creates interest without taking too much time." Foraker thanked him, saying that "the thought upon which you have acted is a very good one and I think much can be accomplished in the way suggested." His only requested change was the word "opulence," a request Houston would appreciate "if you knew how poverty-stricken I am."[40]

No answer is in Foraker's file to the letter, typical of many others, from a J. Silas Harris of Kansas City, Missouri. Harris advised Foraker that without the 50,000 Negro voters of Missouri there would be no Republican party in the state; at least there would be no possibility of the party carrying the state in 1908 without that vote. The blacks, he said, without any organization may not be able to elect a single member of the delegation to the national convention, but they will be able to create a "friendly feeling among those sent for Foraker or they will prevent the election" of the Republican state ticket. "If you desire us to line up for you, you have but to make your wishes known. If you wish to know more of us, we refer you to Colonel R.C. Kerens."[41] No answer exists to this letter, but most of the others similar to it were answered with a conventional expression of gratitude and no commitment.

An unidentified letter to Charles Dick, a member along with Foraker of the conservative wing in leading Ohio Republican circles, referred to the 35,000 Negro voters in Ohio, of whom

> at least 15,000 should be in organized working order before September 1st . . . . if you but properly give me the go-ahead word . . . I can go to Springfield and after eighteen days of diplomatic turning around can make Chairman Krapp and his fifteen committeemen eat crow or take to the woods. . . . We contemplate holding our National Convention in Cincinnati, convening Tuesday, Sept. 17th. . . . We want our closing night to be a Foraker night. . . . It simply takes an earnest and an honest

man who knows his business to do the trick. I think I can fill the bill.[42]

Foraker continued to be indefinite about his candidacy. In June he wrote to Trotter that he had no desire whatever to be a candidate again, "but have stated publicly and privately that I would leave that whole matter to our next State Convention," and thus provided a graceful way to accept the nomination. "When a man has seen as much public life as I have," he said, "it loses its fascination, especially when that which he regards as most unselfish and commendable in his record seems to bring severest criticism."[43] In November, in answer to a letter that began with the words: "From all over this country I have been receiving inquiries as to your candidacy," Foraker said:

> You refer to your last conversation with me in which I told you to give your support to somebody else. . . . I spoke to you then precisely as I felt. I had no desire to become a candidate, and dislike exceedingly to be in such an attitude, but our situation in Ohio seemed to require it.[44]

The same day Foraker posted this answer, a letter to him from William A. Hewlett of Elizabeth, New Jersey, reported that: "We are about to begin work among our colored friends in this part of the state — looking to sending delegates to the national convention who will vote for you or whosoever you may favor for the Presidency of the United States." Foraker did not repudiate the nomination. Instead, he wrote: "All I can say in response to your letter of December 6th is to thank you for its kind expressions and to assure you of my proper appreciation for the same."[45]

George D. Todd of the Todd Manufacturing Company of New Albany, Indiana, in a letter to Foraker early in 1908 offered to organize his state so that "Taft will not get a single delegate from the state" and so that "you get your share of the delegates out of the delegation." He could secure six or eight delegates from Kentucky, "if you desire to do so." Foraker answered that he had such a battle on his hands in Ohio that he had no time for anything outside of his own state, but he left "all such matters to friends who may be able and willing to take up the work and look after it. Any help you can render will be gratefully appreciated,"[46] he concluded.

A detailed and fascinating account from a New York attorney, John Wetmore, described his activities on behalf of Foraker to line up delegates from Florida and Georgia to the convention. The request for his aid and his orders came from Gilchrist Stewart. Wetmore described great support for Foraker among the black voters, even those associated with the Republican machine.[47]

J. Milton Waldron, President of the National Negro-American Political League, sent Foraker a lengthy statement of the activities of his organization and individuals within it who are "unalterably opposed to the Roosevelt-Taft combine, and have been doing all in our power for the last nine months to prevent the nomination of either for the Presidency of the United States." To accomplish this requires, he went on, most, if not all, of the Negro delegates to the national convention, in addition to opposition of "the labor people and the white Republicans throughout the country." Waldron then outlined a program to coalesce the Negro community: use of women's groups, church groups, mass meetings, pressure by established Negro leaders. He ended up with a financial plea. Much more could be done if there were money to employ good speakers. "Since you, as well as we, are vitally interested in this fight, we hope you will see your way clear to help us in a financial way in this matter." Foraker replied that he was too hurried to discuss so broad a subject in a letter, "but I hope I may have the pleasure of making an oral exchange with you."[48]

A few days later Waldron's organization sent out a letter to each Negro delegate opposing the candidacy of Taft or Roosevelt on four grounds: their approval of lily-whitism; their position on Brownsville; Taft's support of disfranchisement amendments; Roosevelt's unwillingness to carry out his party's promise to enact disfranchisement amendments to reduce representation from southern states. A different letter was sent to thousands of individual blacks asking for support for Foraker as presidential candidate.[49]

The end of the fight was quiet. At the National Republican Convention that June, Taft received 702 votes, Foraker 16. He received 8 votes from Georgia, 4 from Ohio, 2 from South Carolina, 1 from Virginia and 1 from the District of Columbia. According to Foraker's biographer, "the Negroes showed their appreciation of the Brownsville case by their votes."[50]

After Taft's nomination, Foraker received much mail suggesting that Bryan would carry Ohio because the Negro vote would never support Taft. Foraker's position on the election was ambivalent. The Dayton, Ohio, Colored League, a Republican organization, urged his help in the campaign; the Republicans could not carry Ohio unless he visited every leading city to encourage black voters to support the ticket. "You can control the colored vote with your advice and if you do not do this Ohio will go Democratic as far as the solid colored voter is concerned. There is eleven thousand here mostly all on the fence so to speak." Foraker's response was grandly bitter: "Am I my brother's keeper?"[51]

Some months later Waldron wrote again to Foraker that "we are doing everything in our power to defeat Taft and the man in the White House and we trust you will do the same. You need only to speak plainly to the Colored people of this country and give them to understand that you feel that they ought to vote against Mr. Taft in the coming Presidential Election, and his defeat is assured." Foraker's reply was noncommittal: "I appreciate very much what you and Mr. Ferguson have done in wiring and writing me," he said, making no substantive reference to the election, but not repudiating Waldron's statement.[52]

Publicly Foraker's position differed. In a statement to B. A. Mack for public release, Foraker said:

> I have been informed by you over the telephone that some one. . . has circulated a story. . . to the effect that I have been writing to colored voters in your county advising them to vote the Democratic ticket. I write to say that if such a story is in circulation it is manufactured out of whole cloth. There is not a word of truth in it. I have not advised anybody, white or black, by letter or otherwise, to vote the Democratic ticket either this year or any other year in your county or elsewhere.
>
> Regretting that there should be an apparent necessity for me to give attention to such an absurd story. . . . [53]

Foraker also issued, though to whom it is not clear, a nine-page memorandum describing his position in relation to support of the Republican ticket. It included reprints of several letters to Republican leaders, who questioned his reticence to endorse Taft publicly. He answered:

> By the action of Judge Taft and President Roosevelt I regard myself as barred from participation in this campaign by either speaking or writing letters for publication. No one can regret this more than I do. . . .
>
> I told him, as I had told the others, that I had never thought of not voting the ticket, that I expected to vote the ticket from top to bottom, not because Mr. Taft was on it, but in spite of that fact, because that was the only way I had of supporting my party and that while Mr. Taft being the candidate and in command of the party for the purposes of the campaign, might eliminate me from the canvass, I denied his right to muster me out of the Republican party.[54]

There is nothing surprising about Foraker's double game. What is surprising is that a seasoned, calculating, shrewd old politician like Foraker thought he could seize the Republican nomination by aligning himself with the pitifully small and ineffective black vote, along with whatever insignificant allied white vote would be attracted to that kind of issue. Could a man so astute so misread public sentiment? Although the first decade of the twentieth century was a period of reform, it was clearly for whites only. Foraker had the better of the argument with Roosevelt but he lost the candidacy. If Foraker was trying to erase the reputation he had as a spokesman for big business, he chose the wrong issue.

Was Foraker operating on the basis of principle or opportunism? To pose the question is to misunderstand the political man, for in him the two are so merged as to be inseparable. Foraker probably could not have been so dedicated to an issue he did not believe in; on the other hand, he probably would not have permitted himself such total commitment if the issue were not what he thought was to his benefit.

Foraker is a difficult man to understand, for even in his private letters and papers his defenses remain intact. He was stiff and high-toned and somewhat pompous, but intellectually penetrating and incisive, publicly and privately. He is described as having fine white hair, but it was rarely let down.

He was a man with a great deal of talent who undoubtedly felt that he had never received the public acclaim he deserved. As far back as 1888, when the Republican convention came to a deadlock between Blaine and Sherman, a significant number of Blaine delegates offered him their support for the nomination, but his commitment to Sherman prevented him from accepting their offer.

> Thereafter fate was against him. He had voluntarily stood aside for an older man; year after year he was compelled to stand aside for younger leaders. . . . Foraker, for all his administrative capacity, his wide popular appeal, and his unflinching courage, had the tragic lot of seeing a succession of associates go above him.[55]

Despite his undeniable talent and skill and his great success, "his unwillingness to compromise with other leaders," his biographer explained, "restricted him from the ranks of Aldrich, Hanna, Lodge, Spooner and O.H. Platt, and placed him just below that all-powerful Senate Group . . . . He could not reconcile himself to the Rooseveltian program."[56] Although his staunch conservatism appealed to a powerful group within the business community, they recognized "that he lacked the qualities of a president."[57]

Is it not possible to view Foraker's commitment to the Brownsville soldiers as his honest attempt to establish a reputation as champion of the oppressed? If the effort failed, as it did, it was largely because Foraker, unused to that pose, did not recognize the right kind of issue with which to reach the American people, and did not, because of his unrelenting, hard-driving manner, have the proper tone to attract a mass following. It was the wrong issue and the wrong style. It was such a botched-up job from an otherwise astute and clever man because it was not his kind of politics.

NOTES

1. By Rev. James D. Corrothers, Foraker papers.
2. Everett Walters, *Joseph Benson Foraker, An Uncompromising Republican* (Columbus, Ohio: The Ohio State Archeological and Historical Society, 1948), p. 4.
3. December 2, 1906.
4. Walters, *Foraker,* pp. 278-79.
5. Roosevelt to Lyman Abbott, May 10, 1908, *Letters of Theodore Roosevelt,* XVI, 1026.

6. *My Quarter Century of American Politics* (New York: Harper & Brothers Publishers, c. 1920), I, 443. General discussion of the Gridiron Dinner affair in the following pages.
7. *Ibid.*, p. 446.
8. *Ibid.*
9. *Ibid.*, p. 448.
10. January 29, 1907.
11. Julia Foraker, *I Would Live It Again: Memories of a Vivid Life* (New York: Harper & Brothers Publishers, 1932), p. 281.
12. *Ibid.*, p. 186.
13. *Ibid.*, p. 289.
14. *Ibid.*, p. 295.
15. *Ibid.*, p. 298.
16. Foraker's secretary, with whom I spoke in Cleveland, said that he had told her that his office had been broken into during the Brownsville investigation and some valuable material stolen. She had not been his secretary at that time.
17. January 1, 1909, Taft papers.
18. *Ibid.*
19. Foraker, *Notes of a Busy Life,* II, 328.
20. *Ibid.*, II, 328–29.
21. June 4, 1907, Foraker papers.
22. December 18, 1908, Foraker papers.
23. Foraker to John T. C. Newsom, March 17, 1907, Foraker papers.
24. Foraker, *Notes of a Busy Life,* II, 233-34.
25. *Ibid.*, p. 246.
26. *Ibid.*, p. 249.
27. *Ibid.*
28. *Ibid.*, p. 251.
29. *Ibid.*, p. 253.
30. *Ibid.*, p. 271.
31. Walters, *Foraker*, p. 245.
32. *Ibid.*
33. Foraker, *Notes of a Busy Life,* II, 313-315.
34. See *ibid.,* II, 312.
35. May 16, 1908, Foraker papers.
36. May 18, 1909.
37. Memo on conversation with Senator Foraker at the latter's residence, Sunday, 6 p.m., December 13, 1908 on stationery of The Commission of the U.S. Government to the Tokyo Exposition, Washington, D.C., Roosevelt papers.
38. Letter to Judge William H. West, May 7, 1909, Foraker papers.
39. Judge West to Foraker, May 7, 1901, Foraker papers.
40. Houston to Foraker, January 1, 1907; Foraker to Houston, January 3, 1907, Foraker papers.
41. March 26, 1907, Foraker papers.
42. May 17, 1907, Foraker papers.
43. June 14, 1907, Foraker papers.
44. L. Henderson to Foraker, November 30, 1907; Foraker to Henderson, December 6, 1907, Foraker papers.
45. W.A. Hewlett to Foraker, December 6, 1907; Foraker to Hewlett, December 14, 1907, Foraker papers.

46. Todd to Foraker, January 3, 1908; Foraker to Todd, January 6, 1908, Foraker papers.
47. Typed report from Wetmore, dated February 7, 1908, with a covering letter to Foraker dated February 8, 1908, Foraker papers.
48. Waldron to Foraker, April 25, 1908; Foraker to Waldron, May 2, 1908.
49. Copies of letters in Foraker papers.
50. Walters, *Foraker,* p. 268.
51. The Dayton Ohio Colored League to Foraker, July 20, 1908; Foraker to the League, July 28, 1908, Foraker papers.
52. Waldron to Foraker, September 29, 1908; Foraker to Waldron, October 2, 1908, Foraker papers.
53. October 24, 1908, Foraker papers.
54. Reprint of letter to J. G. Schmidlapp, October 26, 1908, in *Memorandum*, Foraker papers, typed memorandum, pp. 5, 8.
55. Walters, *Foraker,* Introduction by Allan Nevins, p. ix.
56. Walters, *Foraker*, p. 255.
57. *Ibid.*

CONCLUSION

The Court of Inquiry began the last phase of the Brownsville investigation early in May, 1909. The Court traveled to Brownsville, examined the enormous quantity of testimony previously accumulated and itself heard many witnesses. Eleven months later the Court concluded its investigation. As expected, it found the soldiers of the Twenty-fifth Infantry guilty of the assault upon the town of Brownsville. Although no new evidence was found, the Court asserted that the officers of the battalion might have been able to avert the raid if proper precautions had been taken, and had they not waited until morning to examine the rifles of their men, the guilty persons might have been exposed.[1]

The soldiers were defended by Brigadier General Aaron S. Daggett (retired) as senior counsel and N.B. Marshall, a black lawyer from the Constitution League, as junior counsel.

The Court did not investigate the Boyd Conyers' confession, but in a summary of the case, the following statement was issued:

> the Boyd Conyers confession, according to the preponderance of the evidence, is a bona fide confession, given as stated, and the witness Lawson and the witness Browne are witnesses in good standing before this court. No attempt has been made to impeach the credibility of either.[2]
>
>   .... The confession of Boyd Conyers adds nothing, however, to the evidence. . .as far as it affects eligibility for reenlistment. Most of the names given by Conyers are names that the court could have arrived at

in their classification of men for qualification. However, the confession has been placed before the court, thrashed out at great length, and in spite of the attack made on it, the preponderance of direct and corroborative evidence before the court is to the effect that the Boyd Conyers confession was made as alleged.[3]

The official record of the Brownsville affray was closed on August 13, 1910. Eleven of the fourteen men found eligible reenlisted.[4] No reason was given or shown why these fourteen should have been found "qualified" that did not apply to all the others.

There were many reasons for Foraker and his followers to have feared the amended bill and the subsequent Court of Inquiry investigation established by it. The bill had not stated that all should be eligible to reenlist who were not affirmatively shown to be guilty of the charges; it thus left room for an unfriendly court to so construe the act as to require the men to prove their innocence. Foraker was concerned that if the testimony "fell short of an absolute demonstration," that if the judges were not satisfied that the men were, in the language of the act, "qualified for re-enlistment," they would, without making any affirmation of guilt, deny relief. "What I thus feared is exactly what afterward occurred," he wrote in his autobiography years later,[5] a view of the bill different from that which he expressed at the time. "The inquiry was conducted in a way that would not have been a surprise if the Court had been composed of citizens of Brownsville," he later wrote.[6] Only eighty-two of the discharged soldiers were allowed to testify and appear. There were more than seventy others waiting to be heard when the Court announced that it would not hear any more witnesses.

General Daggett, in his summary argument, reviewed the evidence at length, analyzed it, and offered as a final argument the following: It is a principle of American and English law that a man is innocent till proven guilty. It is an axiom of American and English law that the law will not exact impossibilities. It has been said that these men must prove their innocence. What can they do? How shall they do it?[7]

Marshall, the junior counsel, in a highly dramatic gesture, declined to make any argument, giving his reasons as follows: The oldest and strongest presumption known to the common law of England and adopted by our country is the presumption in favor of innocence. I therefore decline to submit an argument to this Court, he said, for two specific reasons; "First, because the procedure leaves it undetermined whether this Court is a Court of Inquiry or a court martial. Second, because the instructions of the Secretary of War to the Court conflict so fundamentally and totally with my legal training as to make it impossible for me to build an argument which would attempt to prove a negative."[8]

Writing of the episode nine years later, Foraker said that if the Govern-

ment had spent one-tenth part to discover the men who shot up Brownsville
that it did spend to convict its soldiers, the truth would have been established.

* * * * *

It is possible that some of the black soldiers of the Twenty-fifth Infantry
were guilty of the attack upon the community of Brownsville. The Jim Crow
restrictions they found undoubtedly rankled many of the men who had been
born in a part of the country where such restrictions did not then exist.
Among the soldiers were probably several who found accommodation to their
newly prescribed place in society bitter and difficult. These were men, too, of
a kind to be found in a peacetime army, that is rough, essentially rootless,
accustomed to much drinking and carousing for release from the dreariness of
army routine. Freshly placed in a hostile environment, such men might have
reacted by shooting up the town.

It is possible they did not. In spite of its enterprising, entrepreneurial
spirit, Brownsville remained very much a frontier town. The inhabitants were
familiar with firearms. Mayor Combe testified that "the most common
weapon there is the .44 or .45 calibre Colt, as far as pistols are concerned. It
is a hunting country, a cowboy country, and almost every family has arms." [9]

> ... you must remember that Brownsville is the only town in that
> vicinity, and these ranchmen coming in there for a number of miles
> around would ride into town with their six-shooters on. [10]

Brownsville and the surrounding countryside were filled with rough,
rootless, violent men, living in a community as much frontier and western as
it was racist and southern. The town had a more than adequate supply of
saloons and brothels, and both were generously patronized. These bars and
brothels suffered with the arrival of the black troops who could not be
accommodated easily. In general, then, sections of the Brownsville community, too, had cause to be disgruntled.

Is it beyond the limits of reason to imagine certain members of the
Brownsville community incensed enough to place incriminating evidence at
the scene of the shooting, to dress up like soldiers, darken their faces and
shoot up their own town, killing one probably innocent man, just to have the
soldiers driven from Brownsville? Is it more reasonable to assume that the
soldiers, in a planned scheme to shoot up the town, began by calling attention
to their activities before they left the post, and were so careless as to leave
behind incriminating evidence that would immediately implicate them; or
were they so filled with whiskey as to act thoughtlessly? How explain the
unbroken silence of what must then have been the many innocent men who
suffered by their silence? Which Boyd Conyers story should one believe? If
the ballistics and other similar kinds of evidence Foraker presented seemed

impressive, so, indeed was the Government's answer. Was the eyewitness testimony so discredited as to be useless?

If it is not possible to be certain who was responsible for the assault on the town, if Foraker was not able to prove the soldiers' innocence, as he claimed, he did, however, demonstrate that they were not proven guilty. What was decisive in the handling of the entire episode was the unwillingness of the Government investigators to examine the evidence judiciously and to ignore preconceived notions in an effort to treat the troops as men with the right to be heard and respected.

What was also decisive was the unwillingness of Theodore Roosevelt to reopen the investigation with any degree of open-mindedness. Once the debate between him and Foraker was placed in a political setting, for which Foraker was responsible, the issue became a contest between two powerful forces; in the process, the unfortunate men played a relatively minor role. The justice of the case became secondary. Of primary concern were such matters as political ambition, presidential aspirations, threats to authority, executive versus congressional control, intra-party factionalism, personality differences.

While Booker T. Washington's role in the entire affray was a difficult and awkward one, it was not especially honorable either. The dangers inherent in his role of accommodation were highlighted by his reaction to the Brownsville situation. Having entrenched himself in the white community as the moderate spokesman for the Negro, and having learned to enjoy and depend upon the pleasures and rewards reaped from such an association, Washington was unwilling to risk any threats to his position of authority. His response to the Brownsville affray was not motivated as much by the needs of his people as it was by the threat to his, Washington's, power. Undoubtedly had he assumed a critical stance on Brownsville, his relations with Roosevelt and the Republican party, which he had so delicately and carefully established, would have been undermined. His own political power would thus have been threatened, but that his value to the black community, which was ostensibly the reason for his Republican affiliation, would have suffered, is questionable. Perhaps he was sincerely "attempting to bring the wooden horse within the walls of Troy."[11] But in the process, as is always the danger in such cases, he so closely came to identify his private interests with his public ones, that when they conflicted he found himself devoting his energies to maintaining his personal power at the expense of the public, that is the black community's, good.

The black community, genuinely aroused and temporarily united, found no way to channel effectively its expressions of outrage and anger. Its leaders, initially unanimous in criticizing the President's action, ultimately succumbed to mounting pressures that urged return to loyal Republicanism.

When the Brownsville affray was over, Roosevelt and Washington, if they were not unscathed, at least survived; Foraker, risking his career on a bid for the presidency, had lost; and the black community, perhaps a bit more cynical, lapsed into political silence. And the soldiers of the Twenty-fifth Infantry, whose guilt is still in doubt, were permanently penalized when the political controversy that engulfed their little episode was played out.

NOTES

1. *Court of Inquiry Proceedings,* VI, 1634
2. *Ibid.,* 1589.
3. *Ibid.,* 1590.
4. The names of the men reinstated and the dates of their reenlistment are: Edward L. Daniels, May 21, 1910; Edward Warfield, May 12, 1910; Clifford I. Adair, May 7, 1910; Henry W. Arvin, May 9, 1910; Calvin Smith, July 25, 1910; Robert Williams, May 9, 1910; Winter Washington, August 13, 1910; Elias Gant, June 2, 1910; John A. Jackson, May 7, 1910; Samuel E. Scott, May 18, 1910; William Van Hook, May 22, 1910; *Army Service Records, War Department Archives,* National Archives, Washington.
5. Foraker, *Notes of a Busy Life,* II, 314.
6. *Ibid.,* 315.
7. *Argument of Brigadier General A.S. Daggett, U.S.A., Retired, Before the Military Court of Inquiry in the Brownsville Matter,* Washington, D.C. March 23, 1910, National Archives, Washington.
8. Typed statement found in Foraker papers.
9. *Report of the Senate Committee on Military Affairs,* 2405.
10. *Ibid.,* 2429.
11. Meier, *Negro Thought,* p. 116.

BIBLIOGRAPHY

Primary Sources

The Press

Afro-American (Baltimore)
Age (New York)
Alexander's Magazine (Boston)
American Citizen (Kansas City, Kansas)
Arena (New Jersey)
Broad Ax (Chicago)
Brownsville Herald (Texas)
Chicago Public
Cleveland Gazette
Colored American Magazine (New York)
Conservator (Chicago)
Dallas Morning News
Freeman (Indianapolis)
Globe-Democrat (St. Louis, Missouri)
Horizon, a Journal of the Color Line (Washington, D. C.)
Houston Daily Post
Independent (New York)
Indianapolis World
Iowa State Bystander
Moon Illustrated
New Age-Dispatch (Los Angeles)
New York Times
Outlook, a Weekly Newspaper (New York)
Plain-Dealer (Cleveland)
Reporter (Staunton, Virginia)
Republican (Seattle, Washington)
Richmond Planet
Rising Sun (Kansas City, Missouri)
St. Louis Palladium (Missouri)
San Antonio Daily Express
Texas Freeman
Tuskegee Student
Voice of the Negro (Chicago)
Washington Bee
Washington Post
Wichita Searchlight

Manuscripts

Francis L. Broderick notes and papers used in the preparation of his bio-
graphy of W. E. B. Du Bois, at Schomburg Collection, N.Y.P.L.
Joseph Benson Foraker papers, Ohio State Historical Society, Cincinnati, and
Historical and Philosophical Society of Ohio, Cincinnati.
John E. Milholland papers, Fort Ticonderoga Historical Society, Fort Ticon-
deroga, New York.
Theodore Roosevelt papers, Library of Congress.
William H. Taft papers, Library of Congress.
Booker T. Washington papers, Library of Congress.
B. T. Washington-Francis J. Garrison correspondence, Schomburg Collection,
N.Y.P.L.

United States Public Documents

Congressional Record: 59th Cong., 2d sess.; 60th Cong., 1st sess.; 61st Cong.,
2d sess.
Senate. "Hearings Before Committee on Military Affairs, U. S. Senate,"
S. Doc. 402. 60th Cong., 1st sess., Parts 4-6, Serials 5254-5256.
—. "Names of Enlisted Men Discharged on Account of Brownsville Affray,"
S. Doc. 430. 60th Cong., 1st sess., Serial 5256.
—. "Proceedings of a General Court-Martial . . . in the Case of Captain
Edgar A. Macklin," *S. Doc. 402.* 60th Cong., 1st sess., Part 3, Serial
5254.
—. "Proceedings of a General Court-Martial . . . in the Case of Major Charles
W. Penrose," *S. Doc. 402.* 60th Cong., 1st sess., Part 2, Serial 5253.
—. "Reenlistment of Men Discharged Because of Applications," *S. Doc.
430.* 60th Cong., 1st sess., Serial 5256.
—. "Report of the Inspector-General, Message of the President . . . ,"
S. Doc. 389. 60th Cong., 1st sess., Serial 5256.
—. "Report Under Senate Resolution 208," *S. Report 355.* 60th Cong., 1st
sess., Serial 5219.
—. "Reports, Testimony," *S. Doc. 389.* 60th Cong., 1st sess., Serial 5252.
—. "Reports, Testimony," *S. Doc. 402.* 60th Cong., 1st sess., Serial 5252.
—. "Summary Discharge or Mustering Out of Regiments or Companies,"
S. Doc., 155. 59th Cong., 2nd sess., Serial 5078.
War Department. *Discharge of Enlisted Men of 25 Infantry. Brownsville Af-
fray.* Washington: Government Printing Office, 1906.
—. *Employment of Herbert J. Browne and W. G. Baldwin by the War De-
partment at Brownsville, Letter from the Secretary of War, Trans-
mitting, by Direction of the President in Response to Senate Resolution*

of December 16, 1908–a Report. Washington: Government Printing Office, 1909.
—. Inspector-General's Office. *The Brownsville Affray. Report of the Inspector-General of the Army, Order of the President. . . .* Washington: Government Printing Office, 1908.
—. *Names of Enlisted Men Discharged on Account of Brownsville Affray, With Applications for Reenlistment. . . .* Washington: Government Printing Office, 1908.
—. Office Adjutant General. Military Secretary's Department. *Brownsville File.* National Archives.
—. *Summary Discharge or Mustering Out of Regiments or Companies, Letter from Secretary of War Transmitting Additional Testimony and Exhibits in the Brownsville Case.* Washington: Government Printing Office, 1907.

Books

Baker, Ray Stannard. *Following the Color Line: An Account of Negro Citizenship in the American Democracy.* New York: Doubleday, Page & Company, 1908.
Clark, Champ. *My Quarter Century of American Politics.* Vol. I. New York: Harper & Brothers Publishers, 1920.
Constitution League. *Inquiry Relative to Certain Companies of the Twenty-fifth United States Infantry.* 1906.
Cullom, Shelby Moore. *50 Years of Public Service: Personal Recollections of Shelby M. Cullom, Senior United States Senator from Illinois.* Chicago: A. C. McClurg & Co., 1911.
Du Bois, W. E. Burghardt. *Dusk of Dawn: An Essay Toward an Autobiography of a Race Concept.* New York: Harcourt, Brace and Company, 1940.
Foraker, Joseph Benson. *Notes of a Busy Life.* 2 vols. Cincinnati: Stewart & Kidd Company, 1916.
Foraker, Julia. *I Would Live It Again: Memories of a Vivid Life.* New York: Harper & Brothers Publishers, 1932.
Milholland, John E. *Address to National Negro Conferences.* New York: 1909.
Miller, Kelly. *Race Adjustment: Essays on the Negro in America.* New York: The Neale Publishing Company, 1910
— · *Roosevelt and the Negro.* Washington, D.C.: Howard University, 1907.
Proceedings of the National Negro Conference. New York: 1909.
Roosevelt, Theodore. *An Autobiography.* New York: The Macmillan Co., 1916.

—. *The Letters of Theodore Roosevelt.* Selected and edited by Elting E. Morison. Vols. 5, 6. Cambridge: Harvard University Press, 1952.

—. *The Works of Theodore Roosevelt.* 1904.

Scott, Emett, and Stowe, Lyman Beecher. *Booker T. Washington: Builder of a Civilization.* Garden City, N.Y.: Doubleday, Page and Company, 1917.

Terrell, Mary Church. *A Colored Woman in a White World.* Washington, D.C.: Ransdell Inc., 1940.

Articles

Du Bois, W. E. Burghardt. "From McKinley to Wallace: My 50 Years as a Political Independent," *Masses & Mainstream* (August, 1948), 3-14.

Milholland, John E. "Black Suffrage and White Sentiment," *Review of Reviews* (London), n.d.

Mims, Edward. "President Theodore Roosevelt," *Metropolitan Magazine* (New York), XXI (1905), 60-62.

Needham, Harry Beach. *World's Work,* XI (January, 1906), 276.

Page, Thomas Nelson. "President Roosevelt from the Standpoint of a Southern Democrat," *Metropolitan Magazine,* XXI (1905), 68-70.

Williams, C. Arthur. "The President in Texas," *Colliers,* XXV (April 24, 1905), 16-19.

Secondary Sources

Books

Bittle, William E., and Geis, Gilbert. *The Longest Way Home: Chief Alfred C. Sam's Back-to-Africa Movement.* Detroit: Wayne State University Press, 1964.

Blum, John Morton. *The Republican Roosevelt.* New York: Athenium, 1962.

Casey, Robert J. *The Texas Border.* New York: The Bobbs-Merrill Co., 1950.

Chatfield, Lieut. W. H., U. S. Army. *The Twin Cities of the Border.* New Orleans: E.P. Brandao, 1893.

Cutler, James Elbert. *Lynch Law: An Investigation into the History of Lynching in the United States.* New York: Longmans, Green and Co., 1905.

Daniell, L. E. *Texas: The Country and Its Men.* 1917.

Fehrenbach, T. R. *Lone Star: A History of Texas and the Texans.* New York: The Macmillan Company, 1968.

Franklin, John Hope. *From Slavery to Freedom: A History of American Negroes.* 2nd ed. New York: Alfred A. Knopf, 1956.

Ginger, Ray. *The Age of Excess, the United States from 1877 to 1914.* New

York: The Macmillan Company, 1965.

Hale, Annie Riley. *Rooseveltian Fact and Fable.* New York: Published by the Author, 1910.

Hofstadter, Richard. *The American Political Tradition and the Men Who Made It.* New York: Vintage Books, 1956.

House, Edward M., Colonel. *Riding for Texas, The True Adventures of Captain Bill McDonald of the Texas Rangers.* As told to Tyler Mason. New York: Reynal & Hitchcock, c. 1936.

Lee, Alfred McClung, and Humphrey, Norman Daymond. *Race Riot.* New York: The Dryden Press, 1943.

Lewinson, Paul. *Race, Class & Party, A History of Negro Suffrage and White Politics in the South.* New York: Russell & Russell, Inc., 1963.

Logan, Rayford W. *The Betrayal of the Negro: From Rutherford B. Hayes to Woodrow Wilson.* New York: Collier Books, 1965.

Mathews, Basil. *Booker T. Washington: Educator and Inter-racial Interpreter.* Cambridge: Harvard University Press, 1948.

Meier, August. *Negro Thought in America, 1880-1915.* Ann Arbor: The University of Michigan Press, c. 1963.

Moore, Albert Burton. *History of Alabama.* Tuscaloosa: University of Alabama, 1934.

Mowry, George E. *The Era of Theodore Roosevelt, 1900-1912.* New York: Harper & Brothers, 1958.

Murray, Pauli. *States' Laws on Race and Color.* Cincinnati: Woman's Division of Christian Service, Board of Missions and Church Extension, Methodist Church, 1950.

Nordyke, Lewis. *The Truth About Texas.* New York: Thomas Y. Crowell Co., 1957.

Nowlin, William F. *The Negro in American National Politics: 1868-1930.*

Paine, Albert Bigelow. *Captain Bill McDonald, Texas Ranger: A Story of Frontier Reform.* New York: J. J. Little & Ives Co., 1909.

Pierce, Frank C. *A Brief History of the Lower Rio Grande Valley.* Menasha, Wisconsin: George Banta Publishing Company, 1917.

Pringle, Henry F. *The Life and Times of William Howard Taft.* 2 vols. New York: Farrar & Rinehart, Inc., 1939.

—. *Theodore Roosevelt, a Biography.* New York: Harcourt, Brace and Company, 1931.

Richardson, James D., ed. *A Compilation of the Messages and Papers of the Presidents, 1789-1908.* Vol. XV. New York: Bureau of National Literature and Art, 1909.

Richardson, Rupert Norval. *Texas: The Lone Star State.* New York: Prentice-Hall, Inc., 1943.

Rudwick, Elliott M. *Race Riot at East St. Louis, July 2, 1917.* Carbondale,

Ill.: Southern Illinois University Press, 1964.

Schmidt, Theophilus. *A Trip to Texas.* Pamphlet. January, 1910.

Stambaugh, J. Lee, and Stambaugh, Lillian J. *The Lower Rio Grande Valley of Texas.* San Antonio: The Naylor Company, 1954.

Steen, Ralph W. *Twentieth Century Texas: An Economic and Social History.* Austin, Texas: The Steck Co., 1942.

Stephenson, Gilbert Thomas. *Race Distinctions in American Law.* New York: D. Appleton and Company, 1910.

Sullivan, Mark. *Our Times, the United States 1900-1925.* Vol. I, *The Turn of the Century.* New York: Charles Scribner's Sons, 1926.

Tatum, Elbert Lee. *The Changed Political Thought of the Negro, 1915-1940.* New York: Exposition Press, c. 1951.

Texas Almanac and State Industrial Guide 1904. Issued by A. H. Belo & Co. Printed by Clarke and Courts, Galveston-Dallas News, Galveston, Texas, 1904.

Texas Almanac and State Industrial Guide, 1911.

Texas State Historical Association. *The Handbook of Texas.* Walter Prescott Webb, Editor-in-Chief. 2 vols. Chicago: The Lakeside Press, 1952.

Walters, Everett. *Joseph Benson Foraker, An Uncompromising Republican.* The Ohio Governors Series, Vol. I. Columbus, Ohio: The Ohio State Archaeological and Historical Society, 1948.

Woodward, C. Vann. *Origins of the New South, 1877-1913.* Vol. IX, *A History of the South.* Baton Rouge: Louisiana State University Press, 1951.

—. *The Strange Career of Jim Crow.* New York: Oxford University Press, 1955.

Articles

Martinal, Doris. "The Negro Raid," *The History of Teachers' Bulletin,* XIV (no. 1 University of Texas Bulletin, no. 2746, December 8, 1927), 127-33.

Pringle, Henry F. "Theodore Roosevelt and the South," *Virginia Quarterly Review,* IX (March, 1933), 14-25.

Scheiner, Seth M. "President Theodore Roosevelt and the Negro, 1901-1908" *The Journal of Negro History,* XLVII (July 2, 1962). 169-82.

Thornbrough, Emma Lou. "The Brownsville Episode and the Negro Vote," *Mississippi Valley Historical Review,* XLIV (December, 1957), 469-92.

Tinsley, James A. "Roosevelt, Foraker and the Brownsville Affray," *The Journal of Negro History,* XLI (January, 1956), 43-65.

Unpublished Material

Grimshaw, Allen D. "A Study in Social Violence: Urban Race Riots in the United States." Unpublished doctoral dissertation, University of Pennsylvania, 1959.

Levine, Daniel. "Variety in Reform Thought: Social Assumptions of American Reformers, 1890-1912." Unpublished doctoral dissertation, Northwestern University, 1961.

Meier, August. "Negro Racial Thought in the Age of Booker T. Washington, circa 1880-1915." Unpublished doctoral dissertation, Columbia University, 1957.

Tinsley, James A. "The Brownsville Affray." Unpublished Master's essay, University of North Carolina, 1948.

INDEX